Sonia Sotomayor

Sonia Sotomayor
A BIOGRAPHY

BY SYLVIA MENDOZA

ZEST BOOKS

Connect with Zest!

- zestbooks.net/blog
- zestbooks.net/contests

- twitter.com/zestbooks
- facebook.com/BooksWithATwist

2443 Fillmore Street, Suite 340, San Francisco, CA 94115 | www.zestbooks.net

Manufactured in the U.S.A. | 4500645271 | DOC 10 9 8 7 6 5 4 3 2 1

Table of Contents

CHAPTER ONE
Breaking the Curse

"I probably wasn't going to live as long as most people...
So I couldn't afford to waste time."

They said she was cursed. Wondered how she could be a normal kid if she had a disease that could kill her. Wondered if she could have a normal childhood. Asked what would become of her. Asked whether she would die before she made it to high school.

When Sonia Sotomayor was only eight years old, she attended Blessed Sacrament Catholic School in the Bronx, in the heart of New York City. All students had to go to daily Mass at the church next door. One day, in the middle of services, Sonia became woozy. She tried desperately to be quiet and not draw attention to herself. Punishment came to those who misbehaved.

But her vision blurred to the point that the brilliant stained glass windows of the church turned yellow, and then everything went black. She fainted.

She woke to see the nuns looking down at her, with concern etched on their faces. Shivering from fright and from the cold water they had splashed on her face, she lay still and waited for her mother to arrive.

Celina Sotomayor hurried over from work. The worry about Sonia had already been nagging at her, and she knew something might be terribly wrong. Sonia was thirsty all the time, and she also suffered from dizzy spells and blurred vision. She often fainted and wet the bed.

Her body betrayed her over and over, and she was afraid of losing more control. "I was ashamed," Sonia said.

Taking her to the hospital to begin a battery of tests frightened both daughter and mother. When a technician pulled out a needle to draw blood, it was bigger and scarier than any Sonia had ever seen before. The thought of that needle being pushed into her arm was worse than the fainting spells.

She screamed, "No!" and jumped out of the chair and ran. The staff chased her. It was no wonder that she was nicknamed Aji—"hot pepper"—by her family, because she could never sit still. Quick and always moving, her mother said that even at seven months old, Sonia didn't walk or crawl—she got up and ran.

That day at the doctor's office, Sonia—the little aji—used her speed and agility to escape from the staff and blood tests. Fast as ever, she bolted from the room. She raced through the hallways, and once outside, slid under a car and curled into a ball so no one could reach her.

For a few moments, she was safe.

But then one of the staff members—she couldn't see who—grabbed hold of her foot and dragged her out from beneath the car. Fear tore through her and she screamed at the top of her lungs. They carried her back into the hospital nonetheless. Her cries continued when they plunged the needle into her arm later that day.

When the results came in, Sonia's mother sat in the doctor's office while Sonia waited in the hallway. She peeked through the slightly opened door. All of a sudden, her mother started sobbing. Her shoulders quaked.

The tears frightened Sonia. It was the first time she had ever seen her mother cry.

As a nurse who helped others, Celina was a strong woman. She saw the worst of cases, helped the dire in need, and comforted and treated patients who were often incredibly afraid. They relied on her for strength, comfort, and reassurance.

When she saw her mother break down that day, Sonia knew the news couldn't be good. A nurse quickly ushered Sonia from the room so her mother and the doctor could talk privately. Sonia feared the worst. Finally, Dr. Fisher, who had been the family doctor for many years, invited her in.

The diagnosis: juvenile diabetes.

Sonia had type 1 diabetes and would need daily insulin injections.

Diabetes is a disease that prevents a person from being able to process sugar. The cause of type 1 diabetes is unknown, although there does appear to be a genetic factor. Insulin is normally produced naturally in the body to help move the sugar from the blood to cells, and when the body doesn't produce it well enough, people can't get the nutrients that they need from the food they eat. Insulin injections become necessary or else the symptoms become severe—like the ones Sonia suffered from, like being thirsty, wetting the bed, having blurry vision, and fainting. If left untreated, even more severe consequences could result.

Her mother seemed devastated, but Sonia was relieved to finally know what was wrong. Now they could treat her. Now she could get on with her life.

Dr. Fisher shared that he also had the disease, although his was type 2 diabetes. (Although some of the symptoms are similar—including blurry vision, being thirsty, and needing to urinate often—the pancreas continues to produce insulin, so injections are not typically needed.) He reassured her that she could still lead a healthy life if she changed her diet and took her medication. He gave her a sugar-free soda, but after just one sip, Sonia thought it horrible and politely told him no thank you. When he said her diabetes wasn't so bad, Sonia thought, "If it isn't so bad, why is my mommy crying?"

It was bad enough.

In 2016, the Juvenile Diabetes Research Foundation found that more than 3 million Americans had been diagnosed with type 1 diabetes. But in 1962, not much was known about how to treat the disease, especially when it came to children. Complications could include blindness, heart disease, loss of nerve sensation, potential amputations—losing an arm, leg, or foot—or even dying young.

What they did know was that diabetes was going to drastically change Sonia's life.

Even though she was afraid, she decided that the more she knew, the better she would be able to take care of herself. She didn't want to lose an arm or a leg. She didn't want to die.

Sonia lucked out. Taking into account how frightening it could be for a kid, Dr. Fisher answered her questions directly and without hesitation. He was sympathetic to Sonia's turbulent home life. Her disease could cause more heartache and disruption, stress and fear.

He knew there were problems between her parents and how it affected Sonia and her brother. Her mother was a nurse who worked night shift hours, and her father worked as a tool- and die-worker in a factory. He also happened to be an alcoholic.

Sonia wanted to be brave—for herself, her little brother, Junior, and her parents—but it wouldn't be easy. Dr. Fisher was kind and thoughtful, but that didn't prepare her for the types of tests she would have to take at the hospital.

The doctors wanted to observe her because there was still so much to be learned about her disease. For two weeks, Sonia was hospitalized so they could monitor her. She vowed she wouldn't cry, even though the testing hurt and she felt like a guinea pig. They brought in interns to shadow the doctors. They prodded her, put electrodes on her head, dropped new terms. She had no idea what they were talking about.

The grueling process started every day at eight in the morning. A nurse or intern would come in and take some blood. Every half hour they would prick her fingers for a blood sugar reading.

The ordeal was excruciating. After days and days of testing, her fingers and arm were raw and sore. They felt like they were on fire.

To escape the pain, Sonia retreated to her favorite pastime— reading. But she regretted the time she was missing at school. The value of education was already ingrained in her brain. Up until her hospital stay, her mother's unspoken rules included:

never miss work and never miss school. Ever.

So Sonia knew the hospital stay had to be serious. She was an exceptional student who loved to learn and debate, question and seek answers. With that missing, she felt a piece of herself missing, too.

She read for enjoyment and for learning, for a chance to escape her life and for stories to lift her to far-off places. Books did that for her. Dr. Fisher loaned her a book about mythology. In it, she learned of the plight of Greek gods in their many adventures in the vast star-studded skies, depths of the oceans, or across the greenest forest-covered lands. With flaws and traits that seemed more relatable than superheroes, she was taken away to faraway worlds. It was unlike any book she had read, and it sustained her for months.

The best thing she gleaned from the book of mythology, however, was discovering what her name meant. As a version of Sophia, it meant "wisdom." That, she embraced.

She did like to learn. Her favorite books were *Nancy Drew* mysteries though. Seeing herself as a Latina sleuth like Nancy, she was hooked on the adventures. A lover of puzzles, research, and solving problems, Sonia was confident—and determined—that she would make a pretty great policeman or detective someday.

She let the dream simmer in her head, getting her through the worst of times.

Her mother came to visit her in the hospital every day, always bearing gifts. Coloring books, puzzles, and, once, a comic book(!)—which made Sonia especially happy, at least for a while.

Despite the short escapes, the reality of the painful testing broke her spirit.

The last day of the two-week-long hospital stay started like all the others. Her arm and fingers were already burning, and she ached like she never had before. She made it until ten o'clock, but when she saw them lining up the instruments yet again, with the threat of another round of casual torture, she lost it.

"Something inside of me broke," Sonia explained later. "After all those days of being brave and holding it in, I started crying. And once I started, I couldn't stop."

Her mother burst into the room, took Sonia into her arms and shielded her, protecting her from those seen and unseen forces in the room. She held the terrified and sobbing Sonia.

Sonia felt like a cub with her protective lioness mother. Fiercer than ever before, her mother yelled, "Enough! We stop now. She's done."

"She said it in a way that nobody—not the lab technician standing there with the syringe in his hand, not any doctor in Jacobi Medical Center—was going to argue with her," Sonia remembered.

***

Dr. Fisher referred Sonia and her family to the Albert Einstein College of Medicine, a cutting-edge facility for research and treatment that ran a pediatric diabetes clinic. It was located at the Jacobi Medical Center which, thankfully, was in the Bronx, but still a subway ride and bus ride from their home in the

Bronxdale Houses public housing.

Staff taught children how to live with diabetes—learning good nutrition, being aware of their bodies, and recognizing warning signs when blood sugar fell.

Sonia needed daily injections of insulin. Every day she weighed in, took urine samples, and got blood tests. She started to feel like a guinea pig. Worse was the irony of wasting hours and hours in the waiting room at the clinic.

She said, "Did it never occur to anyone at the Albert Einstein College of Medicine that kids who might not have long to live shouldn't have to wait for endless hours with nothing to read but stacks of old *Highlights*?"

Her wry sense of humor and keen sense of observation helped her make the best of her situation. But before long, her pancreas was not producing any insulin at all. If she didn't take her shots, the results would soon be fatal.

Her mother came to the rescue. It helped that she was a nurse, but she also acted like a guardian angel watching over her daughter. With her nursing background, she helped Sonia research diabetes. The more Sonia knew, the more she could take control of her own life and become vigilant and independent.

She also better understood the reality and myths surrounding the disease. True, Sonia had to eat on a strict schedule, but she could actually eat some sweets and could dismiss warnings from her aunts that weren't true—like how eating mangoes could kill her. Not true. She and her mom would often share a piece of cheesecake from the hospital... but only once in a while.

If she overdid it and her sugar spiked, she didn't like how

sick she could get afterward. It felt like a thousand-pound barbell dropped on her lap. The heaviness made her feel like she was moving in slow motion, every movement an effort, making her dizzy and clammy.

So although she and her mother learned about diabetes and her mother helped, but it had not started that way…

Sonia's condition initially affected her home life in negative ways, proving difficult not only for her but for her parents, her brother, and extended family as well. She needed shots every day. They didn't quite know how to help or treat her. Already the situation at home was strained, mostly because of her father's own affliction with alcohol.

Her parents often fought, and now they began fighting over who would give her the shots. They fought about how to give her the shots and whose responsibility it was.

Someone had to give her the injections. That fact made a turbulent situation even worse. When her mother worked night shifts and weekends at Prospect Hospital, her father tried his best to give the insulin shots, but sometimes his hands shook so badly that Sonia was afraid he would jab her and cause more pain than necessary.

Her Abuelita (her grandmother)—her father's mother, whom Sonia idolized—was convinced she was cursed. She blamed the curse on Sonia's mother's side of the family. Yet, she comforted Sonia and tried healing her with herbs and teas brought from the riches of their homeland, Puerto Rico. The concoctions didn't work.

Sonia refused to be cursed. Although she respected her grandmother's traditions and visions, Sonia began to assess her own capabilities. She needed a dose of reality. The reality was that she had a disease. Her belief was that she could gather knowledge and information at her fingertips.

If her parents or Abuelita couldn't give her the dreaded shots, the result would be that her weekly sleepovers at Abuelita's would end. She wasn't about to give up her time with her beloved grandmother. They were like two peas in a pod. And Sonia liked to think she was the favorite grandchild.

One night, while Sonia stood in the kitchen waiting for her parents to finish fighting and give her the injection, she couldn't take her parents' screaming any longer. It was worse than the verdict of being diagnosed. It saddened her to think she was adding to their misery and conflict. Already headstrong and confident, and because she didn't want to be the cause of any more friction between her parents, Sonia decided to take matters into her own hands. She'd had enough.

She dragged a chair to the stove and hopped on it to be able to see the top of the stove. As she studied the burners and knobs, her mother came in and asked what she was doing.

Sonia calmly told her she needed to learn how to sterilize the needle because she wanted to learn to do it herself.

Her mother told her she would burn the house down.

Then she saw Sonia was serious.

That was a lot to ask of an eight-year-old. But if Sonia didn't do it, who would? She wanted as normal a life as she could get. That day, she took control of her destiny and faced her truth: her parents wouldn't always be able to help her. She needed to help herself because she didn't want to rely on anyone else.

And with that, Sonia's mother taught her all she needed to know about the process. Early every morning, Sonia dragged the chair over to the stove, boiled water, and sterilized her needles. She gave herself injections up to four times a day. Also, to get a blood sugar reading, she cut a sliver into her fingertips using a razor blade.

At first, the process was overwhelming. "All the things that you have to do and pay attention to can seem much more than you're capable of… [then] everything becomes second nature very quickly. It's not so tough after a little while," Sonia said later.

Embarrassed by her disease and not wanting to be defined by it, Sonia kept her diabetes secret from everyone else. She didn't want pity. "I didn't want people to think that I was damaged, unclean."

But one day at a party, she suffered a severe sugar low, and her friends grew concerned. That's when she realized her secret could be dangerous—and it wasn't fair when the people she loved most didn't know a vital part of her life and how they could help her. So bit by bit, she started to share her secret with more and more people.

The routine set her on a powerful path, allowing her to be proactive, to face fear, to be focused, and to go after what she wanted because she felt her time on earth might be limited.

The grim reality of the disease—that she could die anytime from complications—still shadowed Sonia. That's when she understood why her mother had cried and her family saw the diagnosis as tragic. Sonia wasn't willing to succumb to those fears and limitations.

Determined to live a normal life, Sonia jumped into adventures and took risks. She studied hard and played hard. She thrived by setting goals that she reached one by one. She explored New York with her cousins, stood up to bullies who terrorized her brother, took dance and piano lessons. Her imagination grew, too.

Reading *Nancy Drew* novels made her dream about picking up cases and solving them like Nancy did. Nancy's father was a lawyer who discussed cases with her. He'd give her tips to solve crimes. Sonia wanted that life and believed she had the very personality and skills she needed:

> "I was convinced I would make an excellent detective, as a keen observer and listener. I picked up on clues, figured things out logically and enjoyed puzzles. I loved the clear, focused feeling that came when I concentrated on solving a problem and everything else faded out. And I could be brave when I needed to be."

One day at the Albert Einstein College of Medicine, she read a pamphlet about jobs diabetics could and couldn't have. She could be a doctor, a lawyer, an architect, an engineer, a nurse, and a teacher.

But what made her pay attention was the list of professions that were "out of bounds" for diabetics.

The list started off with airline pilot and bus driver. She thought that was fair because someone who might pass out and faint shouldn't attempt to fly a plane or drive a bus and put others at risk. Next came the military. Her cousin Alfred had put her and Junior through his own type of boot camp, so she had no desire to pursue that type of career.

Next on the list was police officer. That stopped her. If she couldn't be a police officer, then that meant she couldn't be a detective like Nancy Drew.

There had to be a mistake.

She had all the traits of a successful detective—and they weren't enough.

"I had to go to plan B," she thought.

Plan B came by watching the television show *Perry Mason* every Thursday night. It introduced her to the career of "lawyering."

She didn't know any lawyers. Hardly anyone she knew went to college. But what was important was that lawyers weren't restricted by diabetes. If they could prosecute or defend and do their job well, that's what mattered.

Sonia devoured the show, challenged by the new vocabulary. The courtroom and process to seek justice fascinated her. It was a place where people made a difference. The characters were convincing.

As a defense attorney, Perry Mason untangled the stories behind the crimes, but she liked the prosecutor in the show, too. Los Angeles District Attorney Hamilton Burger thought it more important to find the truth rather than win his case. He believed that if a defendant was truly innocent and the case was dismissed, then "he had done his job because justice had been served."

Most of all, the judge fascinated Sonia. He was the personification of justice, and his decision with a case was the final word.

Court proceedings were like a complex game of finding clues and solving mysteries, highlighting ethical themes of what is right and wrong. She decided she would be either a lawyer or a judge. She didn't know much about either, but she thought both careers might be possible if she worked hard enough.

Like a fearless warrior, she became determined to move toward that goal. Sonia believed what she learned from living with diabetes could actually help her reach her goal.

She learned discipline and internal awareness, and developed a sense of optimism, risk taking, and the awareness that she could ask for help.

Discipline helped her manage her time better. While she waited for the water to boil and the needles to get sterilized, she would brush her teeth, tidy up, and get dressed for school. Later, she was able to apply this discipline to her studies, which made her more likely to achieve the goals she pursued.

Internal awareness meant paying attention to her body and keeping track of when she was getting sick. The most accurate measure was monitoring her body reactions and sensations. Training herself to be super vigilant helped her feel better because she was in control of her own well-being.

This mindfulness and awareness made her more in tune to others, too.

Dr. Elsa Paulsen at the Albert Einstein College of Medicine opened Sonia's eyes to much more than diabetes. Dr. Paulsen was the first woman in an authority position Sonia had ever met. Prior to that, Sonia had only seen the nurses and nurse supervisors at Prospect Hospital where her mom worked, and the nuns at Blessed Sacrament who wielded power over the students but always deferred to the priests.

Watching staff come to attention when Dr. Paulsen walked into a room was impressive. Her bedside manner, her way of talking directly to Sonia and not just her mother, and her genuine care for her gave Sonia a picture of yet another possibility in life: that women could aspire to positions of authority and prestige and still be fair and kind and make a difference.

Sonia rather liked learning from Dr. Paulsen.

Realistic as well as optimistic, Sonia considered her lot in life and how she could react to her disease as either a daily awareness or a limitation. She often considered herself better off than her cousin, Elaine, who was born with a paralyzed arm. Elaine's mother hovered too much, limiting Elaine's potential and capabilities. As a result, she always stayed at the edge of the playground, never able to set foot inside, always watching children play and run in the sand and through the swings.

Sonia didn't want to live that way.

Despite her family's fatalistic view of diabetes, Sonia didn't want to be treated like Elaine, like she was too fragile. She had too much to do. She decided to live and work as though she simply had no time to lose—because, as she figured it, she didn't.

That's when she dedicated her heart and mind to school. She never wanted to miss a day.

She didn't waste any more time. Diabetes wasn't going to hold her back. She could break the curse. Studying hard for years didn't scare her now. She might not be able to become a police officer or a detective, but she wasn't going to let it stop her from pursuing her new dream: practicing law.

She was going to be a Latina Perry Mason.

CHAPTER TWO
Island Girl Values

"The Latina in me is an ember that blazes forever."

Sonia's strength also stemmed from her roots, from somewhere deep inside a tropical paradise, on the island of Puerto Rico. Her family came mostly from the western side of the island, far from the hustle and bustle of San Juan, the capital. Calm, crystalline Caribbean waters added to the majesty of the picture.

The town of Mayagüez, a coastal town, settled by Taínos, initially named "Nuestra Señora de la Candelaria de Mayagüez," is where much of Sonia's family settled. Also known as the "Land of Clear Waters" or "City of the Mangoes," mango trees abound as well as lush, green tropical forests. Agricultural lands once produced coffee and sugar cane. Colorful houses dotted different neighborhoods and the hillsides that offered extraordinary vistas of the turquoise waters below.

In the center of the town, the Plaza de Colón, named after Christopher Columbus, drew the crowds. Festivals and celebrations were held there, but it also served as a place where the community gathered. Colorful storefronts reflected Spanish architecture, like the courthouse and the church that the town was initially named after—Nuestra Señora de la Candelaria.

The black Madonna, patron saint of the Canary Islands, held a candle as if lighting the way. The church faced the square, as if protecting it.

Sonia's Uncle Tito's bakery—a *panaderia y reposteria*, which had been in the family for decades—stood next to the church.

Sonia's family made a name for itself there. But it wasn't always so…

***

Celina Baez, Sonia's mother, was born in 1927, eighteen miles from Mayagüez, in the sleepy village of Lajas. When her own mother died, Celina was only nine years old. Shortly afterward, her father abandoned her and her four brothers and sisters. Under the legal age of eighteen, that made Celina an orphan. For a while, her older sister raised them.

Other family members and their paternal grandmother helped them out. Their generosity with food and staples got them by.

Generations of the Baez family had lived off farmland where coffee and sugar cane crops grew and were great exports for the United States. But hurricanes whipped through and devastated the crop industry, and it never fully recovered. Other jobs outside agriculture were difficult to find. The average income earned in Lajas came in under $8,000 a year—well below the poverty line.

Celina liked to learn, but attending school proved difficult at times. With one pencil in the house to share between the siblings, their mother and father guarded it as if it were gold.

Even though the literacy rate in the town was dismal, Celina seemed determined to use her education to improve her lot in life. Since there were no notebooks to write in, she memorized her lessons and recited them out loud, practicing every chance she could. She often pretended that the few trees outside their humble home were students.

But there was nowhere in Lajas for her to make a decent living. The choices to thrive in their community were slim. Celina saw a dead-end kind of life for herself if she stayed in Puerto Rico.

So she packed her bags, and with fearless drive and a lot of courage—many would later say Sonia inherited this fearless independence from her mother—she left the island at seventeen to join the Women's Air Corps (WAC), a new branch of the U.S. Army at the time. Created during World War II when more help was needed to aid U.S. troops, the WAC recruited two hundred Puerto Rican women.

Assigned to work in Georgia, Celina worked tirelessly to make a life for herself in the mainland United States, despite being alone in a foreign country and speaking only halting English.

Holding fast to her love of Puerto Rican traditions, values, and joy of living, as well as her own values that revolved around education, a strong work ethic, and drive, she made ends meet. With her time served, she left the WAC, and met Juan Sotomayor, another Puerto Rican. During World War II, after Celina was discharged, they dated, fell in love, married, and moved to New York where he got a job as a factory worker. She returned to school to earn her GED, a high school equivalency diploma—and immediately went to work. Her job in the local hospital would later inspire her to return to school to become a nurse.

NUYORICAN SPIRIT

Sonia's father, Juan Sotomayor, had only a third-grade formal education, but he had a knack for math and figuring out problems, a skill Sonia would inherit. With a flair for photography, Juan was also what Sonia called "enormously creative." He read poetry, liked to cook, and created sumptuous dishes like the finest of chefs.

Sonia's parents worked hard to make ends meet. Their extended families moved nearby so that by the time Sonia and her brother, Juan Luis, Junior, were born, their Puerto Rican family flourished in the Bronx.

Known as Nuyoricans—born in New York but with Puerto Rican roots—they looked to their Abuelita Mercedes—her dad's mother—as the matriarch or head of the family. Surrounded by cousins and uncles and aunts, Sonia was raised by the "it takes a village" mentality, but had a special connection with her grandmother and often found a safe haven with her.

In a time when disparity and racism raged in the 1960s and '70s, being Nuyorican sometimes proved difficult. Sonia found comfort in knowing that strength in family and tradition could transcend racial tensions. Despite the hardship of dealing with poverty in the city, together they were strong.

The joy of the island music—in dance like salsa, or in the unique instruments like the guiro and maracas—gave them a beat to live by. With that rhythm in their hearts, clear values, and traditions, they knew, at least at home, they were safe.

The beauty of the Spanish language and Puerto Rican culture came to life in family get-togethers. Even though the palm trees and crystal-blue waters were missing, island generosity and tradition was brought into the Bronx when Celina opened their apartment home to Sonia's friends and gave them a safe place to come and hang out. She cooked them Puerto Rican food like plates of pork chops, *arroz y gandules y pernil*, *mofongo*, and other delights, which were eaten at countless family get-togethers, holidays, and special events. All the while, heavy discussions could be had, or music could be playing. Sometimes Sonia's friends sat side by side with her Titi Aurora, watching television and singing commercial jingles in Spanish.

On Saturdays, the women would gather in their little apartment kitchens and shoo the kids out. Sonia's aunts and grandmother would bring the vitality and island living to life by cooking up *sofrito*—a homemade seasoning of tomatoes, garlic, onions, tomatillos, and a variety of green, yellow, and red peppers—all day long, amid music, laughter, gossip, eating, and loving, lively exchanges. The festivities gave a sense of family and love.

Sonia wanted to hear every word as they chopped vegetables, talked, laughed, and exchanged gossip. Sonia pressed her ear against the kitchen door to hear. She wanted to be a part of that link of womanhood, of that link to her heritage, of that link to two worlds. Sometimes in school or on the street, Spanish was treated as though it were inferior to English. Then and there in the kitchen, with her family, all she could hear was the singsong lilt of a beautiful language that she was privilege to and it didn't sound foreign. Being able to speak both was suddenly a blessing.

After those Saturday family dinners—which often also included games of dominoes or cards—they'd clear the table to get down to Sonia's favorite part of the evening: when Sonia's grandpa and grandma would read poetry out loud. Mostly they seemed to read to each other, but even so, it was inspiring and even romantic. It seemed to transport them back to the island. The recitals educated Sonia about her culture, brought it to life, and brought her much joy.

HOLDING ON TO THE ISLAND BREEZE

And so even though Puerto Rico was thousands of miles away, it gained a place in Sonia's heart via the poetry of her grandparents and the rhythm of each musical note played in their homes. The spirit of their culture and island living was brought to life by dance or by instruments like guitarras, guiros, cuatros, and maracas.

On visits to the island, Sonia connected with her roots and began to realize what made it special. In Mayagüez—only two hours from San Juan, but it felt like a world away with its relaxed flow of beaches and lifestyle—she found peace and connection with her roots. Even with American industries setting up shop in the commonwealth, Sonia didn't see the political or economic difficulties there, only the warmth of the sunshine and love of her family.

The rainforests and tropical feel, mangos fresh from the trees, and piraguas—snow cones—for hot summer days were what Sonia remembered. When she closed her eyes, she might picture the little *coqui*—the tiny island frog that could sit on a fingertip.

The diverse beauty of the island laid the foundation for living in the wonderful world in which she was beginning to find a home. Being bicultural meant she was being raised with two worlds at her fingertips.

She was lucky to speak pretty decent Spanish, but her brother, who was three years younger, didn't speak much Spanish at all. Sonia couldn't dance salsa or keep a beat, and she thought that was embarrassing for a Latino household, but her cousins, on the other hand, were naturals and could dance the night away. It made her realize that every Latino has a different experience and helped her not stereotype others.

Sonia later said, "Although I am an American, love my country and could achieve its opportunity of succeeding at anything I worked for, I also have a Latina soul and heart, with the magic that carries."

CHAPTER THREE
Sonia from the Bronx

"Although I grew up in very modest and challenging circumstances, I consider my life to be immeasurably rich."

Sonia was born on June 25, 1954, in the heart of the Bronx in New York City at Flower Fifth Avenue Hospital, where her grandma, Abuelita Mercedes, would die more than forty years later. Born in New York but with Puerto Rican roots, Sonia was instantly a Nuyorican.

Tall redbrick buildings, one after another, lined her street. Known as the projects, the apartments were government-subsidized housing for poor or low-income households. Sonia's family lived in a tenement and later moved to the Bronxdale Houses, on the better side of town. This was the place where Sonia's parents intended to raise their children, a new co-op neighborhood. In an affordable housing co-op, people can invest in and own a share of the apartment buildings with a down payment and monthly rent payments and get a tax break, too. The more invested they are in their community, the more likely they are to help keep it up. That's the idea, anyway.

Back then, the Bronxdale Houses were public housing for working-class families moving up, a few miles from Yankee Stadium. To live in these projects during the 1950s and 1960s was a dream come true, but that's not to say that everything was perfect. People from all walks of life ventured to the area. There were a variety of different ethnic and religious backgrounds represented. The people who lived there enjoyed what the community had to offer—good schools, parks, stores, libraries, a post office, a fire station, and restaurants.

Still, danger lurked nearby.

"There were working poor in the projects," Sonia said. "There were poor poor in the projects. There were sick poor in the projects. There were addicts and non-addicts and all sorts of people, every one of them with problems, and each group with a different response, different methods of survival, different reactions to the adversity they were facing. And you saw kids making choices."

One of those kids was Nelson, Sonia's cousin, who was more like a soul mate. Sonia saw him get lured into drugs as they grew older and saw his potential disintegrate. He fell into the negative statistics of the Bronx. The images in movies, the news, or on television gave the impression that the Bronx was gang- and drug-infested. Sometimes the image was not far from the truth.

Of the five boroughs in New York, the Bronx stood out for three things: it had the most Latinos—mostly Puerto Ricans and Dominicans—the biggest Spanish-speaking population, and the highest poverty level. The Bronx contained one of the five poorest Congressional Districts in the United States, but it also included some of the most affluent, including upper- and middle-income neighborhoods such as Riverdale, Fieldston, Pelham Gardens, Morris Park, and Country Club.

In the late 1960s and the 1970s, there was a sharp decline in livable housing and quality of life. Challenges always reared up. Temptations to go down the wrong path when both parents worked, like Sonia's did, in order to put food on the table and a roof over their heads, could be found at every street corner.

Sonia never thought of herself as a minority because most of her neighborhood was Hispanic. Puerto Ricans in her neighborhood had a pioneering spirit, presumably because they left worse tenements or poverty back on the island. Sonia became adept at learning street smarts and survival skills as she maneuvered Southern Boulevard, "the center of her childhood universe." Seeing the very best of both worlds—American and Latina—is what Sonia loved most about her life in the Bronx. But she had to stay on her toes—and luckily she also had her family to protect her.

FAMILY INFLUENCE

Surrounded by a strong-willed mother, a large extended family, and Puerto Rican roots that meant family was in her business, Sonia was accountable for every day of her young life. There was nothing she could do or say that wouldn't get back to her family. As a girl in that time and place, she had curfews and chaperones. Sonia took it as a matter of fact and didn't mind. Sonia played with her many cousins and friends. If they roamed the streets, come nightfall, there was always curfew: she had to be indoors by a certain time.

Her boy cousins, however, had fewer restrictions—and could get into more trouble.

Her cousin, Nelson, was like a brother to her. Because she was a girl, she couldn't go outside like he could. Over time, he got caught up in the world of drugs. Watching him spiral into that darkness brought a great deal of pain to the family and to Sonia, who felt helpless.

While they were young, however, there was excitement of living on those streets, too, and bringing the best of her Puerto Rican roots to life with her New York City home. In the Bronx, the lilt of Spanish punctuated the air everywhere they went.

The best thing was living in close proximity to the rest of her family. She and her cousins walked to her abuela's apartment, which was always brimming with heavenly smells of Puerto Rican food. They sat at the window in her apartment and made faces at people getting on the elevated No. 5 train. They also ventured out to watch Spanish movies starring the Mexican comedian *Cantinflas*. Even though he was not Puerto Rican, he brought a certain pride and connection to Hispanic communities.

Sonia loved hanging out with her grandma. Her abuelita believed in God and family, just like Sonia; but she also believed in traditions and curses and natural remedies, and often believed that she could cure Sonia's diabetes.

Parties at her grandmother's were lively, with dozens of family members crammed into small apartments, eating mounds of delicious Puerto Rican food. A Yankee game could vie for airtime, playing loudly on television in the adjoining living room, while the lovely beat of salsa and merengue music blared from open windows. The richness of this culture was sometimes lost on others who weren't familiar with Puerto Rican living.

THE STRUGGLE AT HOME

Sonia's parents were hard workers. While her father worked at the factory, her mother worked as a telephone operator at Prospect Hospital, a small private hospital in the South Bronx. Later she received her practical nurse's license and continued to work as a nurse.

Her parents' financial struggles—and personal problems—forced Sonia to be a caretaker to herself and her brother. Sometimes Junior got on her nerves though. One day, she'd had enough. She took him by the hand and led him outside to the hallway—and left him there. She went back into the apartment and locked the door behind her. He stayed in the hallway until her parents came home—and then she got in trouble for it.

But if he or any of her friends were ever picked on by others at school or in the neighborhood, she wouldn't stand for it. Sonia couldn't stand bullies and always stood up for the underdog. Though Junior could be annoying, Sonia believed only she was allowed to pick on him. Even though they were poor, her family ensured that Sonia knew that everyone had to support everyone else. They had each other's backs.

Her extended family watched out for her when her hardworking mother and father couldn't be there for her and Junior. Though overworked and worried about the money to keep sending Sonia and Junior to Catholic school, Celina and Juan were willing to make sacrifices to give their children an opportunity to have a better education. Yet it took a toll.

All Sonia could remember of her father and mother was

their fighting. It wasn't until she was much older that she learned that there had been a true romance at one time.

Sonia knew her father suffered. His hands shook, which was one reason he couldn't give her the insulin injections she needed in the first place. She learned he was an alcoholic. It was difficult to live with someone with an addiction like that because it became the addiction of the family. The pain of the needle wasn't as bad as hearing her parents argue or seeing her father hurt.

The whole situation became a turning point in Sonia's life. To escape the fighting of her parents, she disappeared to her room to read. Whether it was to dive deep into her studies or into the faraway, make-believe worlds of *Nancy Drew*, she grew independent and found comfort in books and learning. Sonia knew in her heart that her parents loved her, but the sadness they caused was also real.

She imagined a different life for herself. She pictured herself alongside Nancy Drew-like a sidekick, solving mysteries, being a sleuth, acting as the best of detectives because she had a good mind and could solve problems logically. She loved TV, too, especially comedies like *I Love Lucy* and *The Three Stooges* and dramas like *Perry Mason*. Her studies became a productive escape.

Sonia later said, "I have always felt that the support I've drawn from those closest to me had made a decisive difference between success and failure… Whatever their limitations and frailties, those who raised me loved me and did the best they knew how."

FATHER'S DEATH DEVASTATES THE FAMILY

One day, coming home from school, Sonia was greeted by her uncle with a somber face. He brought her and Junior to their aunt's home where her mother and others were crying, and immediately Sonia knew it was her father. He had died from complications to his heart problems, made worse by his affliction with alcohol.

He was only forty-two. Sonia was nine years old.

Juan's death devastated Sonia and her family. They all gathered at Abuelita's house. Her grandma had a deep belief in the spirit world, which scared Sonia and her cousins, but they respected her as she tried to communicate with that other world. She led in prayers to send her son into the next world but to keep his spirit close. And although Sonia didn't believe in that part of her abuela's spiritual practices, it brought her some comfort.

And so she grew up fatherless for the rest of her formative life. Celina became a single mom, raising Sonia and Juan Luis, Junior, alone. With no savings stored away, she began working six days a week. Sonia and Junior's school, Blessed Sacrament, gave them a two-for-one deal and allowed Celina to pay less for tuition, which helped keep the children in Catholic education. The nuns seemed to disapprove of the family's situation, frowning on women who worked outside the home, but her mother pressed forward.

"The irony of course was that my mother wouldn't have been working such long hours if not to pay for the education she believed was the key to any aspirations for a better life," said Sonia.

Struggling with two jobs, and trying to deal with her grief, Celina grew distant and pulled away from Sonia and Junior. For a while, it felt as if Sonia had lost both parents until she finally told her mother to "knock it off."

Then Celina Sotomayor became the role model Sonia needed.

THE ROLE MODEL

After Sonia's father died, her mother had to hustle. She realized she was alone and had to make a living and raise two young children. Besides working two jobs, she went back to school so that she could become a nurse and earn a better living.

Once she reached that goal, Sonia's mother worked all day as a nurse to support Sonia and her brother. (She also helped the people in their building and in the neighborhood.) She was glad she already had a profession where she could support Sonia, but she wanted Sonia to support herself.

Sonia didn't need much convincing.

Sonia's mother knew the importance of an education and of dreaming big. Sonia and Junior never messed around with or questioned their mother's requirement that they never miss school or work. Sonia hated to miss school, but it was unavoidable when she was diagnosed with diabetes. That was the longest absence she had ever had from school. Her mother, meanwhile, urged them to speak more English—and speak it better.

Watching her mother raise them gave Sonia a sense of independence. She focused more on her brains than on her looks—she actually always looked a little unkempt, with her unruly hair, her blouse sticking out of her school uniform, and her shoelaces untied. Luckily, getting into mischief and being sent to the principal's office didn't deter her from her love of education and learning either.

Education was the highest priority. Celina saved enough to buy her children an *Encyclopedia Britannica*, a novelty in the projects—and became famous for the encyclopedia set. They opened a new world for Sonia, her brother, and their cousins and friends in the projects. The books offered hours of delight and research, awe and fascination.

Sonia always knew she would have an occupation. Not just a job, but a career. Her mother's drive helped her see the important steps to get there. Celina knew that Junior would go to college because it was a natural assumption and a sign of the times that boys did and girls didn't; but she pushed Sonia to go, too.

After years of nurturing her thirst for knowledge, Sonia was as solid in her intelligence as she was comfortable in her own skin. She could open up and share herself with others, whether it was about her diabetes or with the compelling issues of the day. "I think there is some comfort in liking yourself enough to be comfortable in your own world," she said.

Sonia's world then revolved around the Bronx, embracing her bicultural Nuyorican life. With a forward-thinking mother guiding her though, education would lift her as an independent, self-sufficient woman with a purpose that would take her far beyond, to another world she only imagined.

CHAPTER FOUR

Star Student: Launching the American Dream

"My mother taught us that the key to success in America is a good education."

If there was one thing about Sonia, it was that she wasn't afraid to ask questions. She learned that from her mother. She had a natural curiosity, although some mistook it for disrespect.

Even though she was one of the best students at Blessed Sacrament, the nuns were sometimes shocked by her willingness to ask questions. In those days, women weren't supposed to ask questions, especially of authority figures.

Maybe that came from her mother, whose resourcefulness and work ethic burrowed into Sonia. She didn't take no for an answer, and she always sought solutions to a problem.

Attending a Catholic school meant sacrifice for families like Sonia's, but her mother was determined, especially once her father died, to keep Sonia and Junior educated and on the straight and narrow.

Sonia watched her mother struggle working at a hospital

and attending nursing school at the same time. Going back to school was a challenge in and of itself. Celina often lamented that the tests were too difficult, that she wouldn't pass them, and Sonia in return would lose patience with her and say if her mother stopped studying, then so could she and Junior. But somehow, Celina always passed with flying colors. They actually ended up studying side by side.

The set of *Encyclopedia Britannica*, which Celina saved and scrimped for, lit a fire in Sonia and Junior. They read the books constantly, devouring the material, learning intricate details about insects and countries, literature and history, philosophers and politicians; it was like a virtual movie theater at their fingertips. Anything they wanted to look up, they could. Some entries even had pictures. Sonia read everything she could get her hands on. The whole apartment complex was in awe.

Books had been her escape from poverty and from pain, especially when her dad died. They shut out the noise, and what she found in books took her to lands far from her world. She said, "I understood there was more I could dream to do and see."

The three books that meant the most to Sonia were the Bible, Shakespeare's complete works, and *Don Quixote*. The Bible inspired her to be the kind of person she wanted to be; Shakespeare offered insights into human nature; and *Don Quixote* reminded her of "the spirit of the chase," of following your dreams.

"…I do think there's a need to be idealistic. … I would rather live a life being hopeful than not, dreaming rather than giving up," she said.

The love of reading set her up for success at her schools.

CATHOLIC SCHOOLS VS. PUBLIC SCHOOLS

Sonia's family, like many other working-class Puerto Rican families in the Bronx, saw public schools as too rowdy and dangerous. Since the Sotomayors were Catholic, Celina and Juan had worked several jobs to pay the tuition for Sonia and Junior at the Blessed Sacrament Elementary School and Cardinal Spellman High School in the Northeast Bronx.

Founded in 1929, Blessed Sacrament was so close to the Bronxdale Houses that the brick building complex could be seen from the school's playground. Older students attended school in upstairs classrooms inside Blessed Sacrament Church. Younger ones had classes in a building behind it. Fewer than three hundred students attended during the regular academic year. Of those, the majority were Hispanic. Girls outnumbered boys. Once the neighborhood was mostly middle-class, but over time graffiti slashed across the walls of nearby homes and storefronts. This indicated that the neighborhood might not be as safe as it once was.

Some graffiti is made by gangs and taggers to mark their "territory" with specific paint symbols, scrawls, and words. This kind of tagging can lead to confrontations and violence. Often, tough economic times can lead to desperation—if there is a lack of jobs and opportunities, drugs and crime can settle into once sought-out neighborhoods.

For Sonia's childhood, she was relatively safe if she stayed within her neighborhood. Sonia attended Blessed Sacrament in the 1960s, from kindergarten through eighth grade, with forty to fifty students in each grade. Up until fifth grade, Sonia was a C student. Then the nuns started giving out gold stars—and her competitive nature emerged. She studied hard but when she couldn't "get it," she asked a superstar classmate who earned many gold stars how *she* studied. Sonia wanted to earn those gold stars, too, and set off on a mission to do so.

Even though she loved school, the rule-bound nature of a Catholic education pitted her curiosity and natural tendency to ask questions—too many questions sometimes—against authority. Even in third grade, she dreaded being disciplined by the black-robed Sisters of Charity, who would take her to the principal's office or punish her in other ways.

"Discipline was virtually an eighth sacrament," said Sonia.

Trouble seemed to find her. Sometimes she asked questions that shouldn't be asked. Other times she seemed to cause offense by simply trying to puzzle things out. Once, when the nuns at her school told her to finish eating a piece of rye bread on her plate, she told them she didn't want to. They told her there were starving children in India.

Sonia told them, "Well, I'll mail it to them."

Hauled up to the front of the cafeteria, she was slapped. "Everyone saw me get punished for the smart mouth that I had," she said.

Sonia was also occasionally sent to the principal's office for saying things out of turn. Her mother would have to pick her up there.

What Sonia learned that day in the cafeteria when she was punished in front of everyone was a lesson in humility. She learned that there were always people more needy than herself and that she had an obligation to think of them. Over time, she came to believe that God was good and "his intent was to help human beings become better people."

Catholic school taught her that sometimes there is a need to follow strict rules and that authority matters. Discipline guided Sonia, and compassion for others took root in her heart and mind.

In 1968, with a near-perfect attendance record, Sonia graduated at the top of her class.

CARDINAL SPELLMAN HIGH SCHOOL

In high school, her thirst for knowledge expanded. And she found herself attending Cardinal Spellman Catholic High School, founded in 1959, which had earned a reputation as a school for high achievers. She was in the right place.

In school, she focused on social issues, turning the spotlight on the plight of others. She stood up for what was right and questioned when something seemed wrong.

It helped that her best friends were bright and challenged her. Other students were also drawn to her, perhaps because Sonia was very good at listening. She would find friends confiding in her and seeking her out for advice. And many of those personal conversations took place at Sonia's home. Her mom would cook while Sonia and her friends discussed issues of the day, like protests over the Vietnam War or difficulties with homework in math class.

Ken Moy, one of her best friends, had a dad who was a gambler with drug problems and a violent temper. Studying gave him an escape from his troubled home. They studied philosophy and belonged to many clubs together.

In addition to being a close friend, Ken was also the student coach who helped Forensic Club students with debate and speech. Forensics Club at Cardinal Spellman was good training for a career in law. Sonia has described the twelve girl members as "self-selected, high-functioning nerds." The club followed a pre-professional program that trained members in public speaking and debate skills.

Each team member was handed a topic and had to argue a pro or con side without emotional attachment, although the goal was to elicit emotion from the audience. It didn't matter what the member believed about the issue she was assigned; what mattered was how well she could make her case. To prevail, a team member had to be able to argue both sides, to listen well, and to think like the opposition, too.

"I was amazed that something so mathematically pure and abstract could transform into human persuasion, into words with the power to change people's minds," said Sonia.

Ken served as their student mentor and she thought him brilliant—until he told her not to talk with her hands. She was astounded by this. "Tell a Puerto Rican not to talk with her hands? Ask a bird not to fly."

Sonia enjoyed exploring and testing ideas, and was inspired by the atmosphere of thoughtful, stimulating conversation and heated debate. One time, she had to debate with an animated girl who spouted Marxist theory.

At one point, Sonia sensed her opponent getting annoyed. When time was up, Sonia asked her why she'd turned so angry. The girl felt Sonia didn't take a stand. "…Everything depends on context with you. If you are always open to persuasion, how can they tell if you're friend or foe? The problem with people like you is you have no principles."

The accusation took Sonia by surprise, but in reality, the interchange made her look inward. She actually did have a solid belief system. Basically, she believed that sometimes a responsible person has to think about all sides of a situation, really assess the facts and take into consideration circumstances that affect individuals and their decisions. She never wanted to assume things about individuals or stereotype them, but there had to be some inner principle that drives them to make choices.

The core lesson for Sonia never wavered however, and that interaction convinced her that a person without principles is also necessarily a person who, in her words, "has no moral core."

THE DOUBTERS

In the 1970s, the Women's Movement and Civil Rights Movement challenged authority and stereotypes. Affirmative action gave people of color a chance to get access to higher education and better employment opportunities. For Sonia, this meant a better chance of going to college.

People of authority—teachers, for example—questioned her knowledge and drive. One of the nuns at Blessed Sacrament wrote in her yearbook that Sonia aspired to be both a lawyer and a mother—and questioned whether she would be able to do both.

It was as if she had to prove herself twice every time, over and over, when people doubted her for not having what it took to be at the top of her class, especially as a Latina.

Her high school math teacher couldn't believe that she was able to pass the test with such a high score. Sonia was asked to retake the exam. She did.

Sonia almost took it as a matter of course that she would have to retake tests because those in authority doubted her—but she didn't doubt herself or her capabilities. She didn't really mind that she had to be put to the test over and over again.

When she retook the math test in question, she again found herself at the top of her class, with higher scores than her white counterparts. This would not be the only time she was asked to take tests over. And it would not be the only time she proved people wrong. She was once asked how she could score higher than the Caucasian students who applied to the Ivy League schools.

Sonia shrugged. "I do know one thing about me," she later said. "I don't measure myself by others' expectations or let others define my worth."

But it seemed she was viewed as something of a threat to people who didn't know her. Many such people perceived her as "less than"—less important or valuable because of the color of her skin or because she was a woman or because she was poor, or because of where she came from. Every chance she could, Sonia corrected them. "That's not who I am," she would say.

Her pride didn't waver. That pride extended beyond academics.

Dating her high school sweetheart, Kevin Noonan, was almost like being put to another test. Inseparable after their first date in Manhattan, they became best of friends, enjoying each other's company while challenging each other academically. Because she was Puerto Rican, his mother did not like her. As time passed, they grew more comfortable with each other. Sonia's mother saw Kevin as another son. The unspoken rule for many Catholic families—that you married your high school sweetheart—seemed to be in effect here, despite the fact that Kevin's mother wasn't especially fond of Sonia. The question was whether they would marry right after high school or after college. They waited.

Being a student at Cardinal Spellman pushed her to standards of academic excellence and also to spiritual awakening, giving her moral values and a basic sense of right and wrong. She also believed that being raised Catholic taught her compassion. "I think being a Catholic made me a better person. It taught me how to choose good over evil, and how to be a more caring human being."

Sonia graduated from Cardinal Spellman High School as valedictorian of the class of 1972. She learned to really listen to what people had to say, to understand and argue both sides of an argument. She tried her luck at persuading others, which would help her in her life as an attorney. She was a student activist and in student government. All were good traits that would later help her on her path toward being a judge.

Outside of school, Sonia was inspired to stay on her path in other ways. When Senator Robert Kennedy came to the Bronx, she was moved by his words for social justice and civil rights. When he was later killed, Sonia decided to follow in his footsteps and made a vow to continue his mission.

Heading into the unknown, almost unbelievable world of Ivy League colleges could have been a frightening experience, a different world from anything she'd ever known or imagined, but she was on a mission. Social justice would guide her.

CHAPTER FIVE

The Fairy Tale Land of the Ivy League

"I honestly felt no envy or resentment, only astonishment at how much of a world there was out there and how much of it others already knew."

Sonia's friend Ken graduated from Cardinal Spellman High School a year ahead of her and was the first of her friends to be admitted into Princeton University. He urged her to apply to an Ivy League school, too. They had challenged each other academically all through high school, had challenged each other to think critically about social issues and world events, and had challenged each other to present perspectives logically and with conviction ever since they were in Forensics Club together. He believed in Sonia's skills and that she would be an excellent candidate for an Ivy League school.

Sonia didn't know what "Ivy League" meant. As a good researcher and student, however, she was confident enough that she had a good enough chance to get into a particular kind of school as anyone else.

She soon learned that Ivy League is an officially trademarked name for a series of colleges on the East Coast. Harvard, Yale,

Princeton, Penn, Brown, Cornell, Dartmouth, and Columbia are the schools that make up the Ivy League. Their names are linked to unparalleled prestige and rigorous academic standards of excellence. (Originally, the "Ivy Agreement" was created to improve intercollegiate athletics, like football.) Tuition and expenses could add up to more than $100,000 for four years, making it difficult to afford. Many believed only the wealthy could afford to attend an Ivy League school.

When Sonia was ready to go to college, it was the time of affirmative action. Affirmative action was a federal policy that gave people of color an improved (and, people argued, fairer) chance at education or jobs that they might not have had otherwise. Employers and universities were supposed to offer equal opportunity programs.

In a 1965 speech, U.S. President Lyndon Johnson explained how affirmative action was an attempt at fairness and antidiscrimination. He gave the example that after African Americans had been liberated from slavery, they needed a hand up, a little extra help to get better-paying jobs to eventually give back to their communities. He believed that if they were brought to the starting line of a race—if they applied for a job—they couldn't compete for certain positions because, up until that point, they wouldn't have had the skills training or education necessary to get a foot in the door. It wouldn't be fair. Affirmative action resources could help even the playing field.

Many say affirmative action gave Sonia a foot in the door to a solid education into an Ivy League school because otherwise she wouldn't have been admitted. Affirmative action programs didn't guarantee success though—that was up to each individual person.

Calling herself an affirmative action baby, Sonia jumped at the opportunity to further her education. She applied to several Ivy League schools.

The movie of the year in 1970 was *Love Story*, starring Ryan O'Neal and Ali MacGraw. What captivated Sonia was the college campus that was featured: Harvard University. The film romanticized love, yes, but it also romanticized the school. It looked like a dream, a fairy tale land of what she imagined a college should look like.

The film featured "pristine snowy fields… a cathedral of learning whose denizens lived out what seemed like an antiquarian fantasy, debating under pointy arches, scaling book-lined walls and lounging on leather couches."

So she applied to Harvard.

Many years later, she would learn that the movie was actually filmed at Fordham University—in the Bronx—not far from where she lived. Had she known that, she might not have left her home turf. The power of the image of Harvard lured her from the comfort of home. She knew she had to leave.

The fairy tale land of the Ivy League was unlike anything she had ever seen. The manicured lawns were greener than any park she'd ever played in, and the grass ran for what seemed like miles. The buildings, although they had been around for generations, didn't look anything like the rundown projects that were only a few years old and falling apart already.

The minute she stepped onto the Harvard campus to be interviewed for admission to the university, it was like she was under a microscope. Nothing felt right. She went into the president's office waiting room and knew in her gut for the first time that she didn't fit in. That this was all wrong for her.

The well-groomed, gracious secretary greeted her nicely enough in her black dress and pearls. But even in her best clothes and with her best manners possible, the vast difference between Sonia and this world paralyzed her. The white couch, the intricate Oriental rug, the two little lapdogs that seemed to stand watch over the room all made her feel out of place. They seemed to make a mockery of her.

She panicked.

Suddenly paralyzed with fear, she didn't know what to say. She didn't feel like could pull it off. So she ran away—literally ran away—from this terrifying situation. (But it was to be the last time that she would choose to flee.) Before she could be interviewed. Before she could convince them she deserved to be there. Before she could see herself as a student in the beautiful school that promised her a future better than any she imagined.

The Ivy League schools her friends spoke of might just as well have been mountaintop castles—unattainable visions of a better and more beautiful world. They existed in an alien landscape far from her Bronx home. They were nothing more than a fairy tale, a fantasy. And maybe that dreamscape just wasn't for her.

Sonia returned home and told her mother what had happened. They didn't dwell on it too much. Her mother stayed positive and believed Sonia would find the right college where she would feel comfortable yet challenged. There were other Ivy League schools besides Harvard to choose from. Eight in all.

Maybe like Goldilocks in that fairy tale, Sonia just had to find the college that was "just right" for her. She had run from Harvard. She visited Yale, but protests dotted and disrupted the campus. She just wanted to get ready for her interview. It felt too progressive for her conservative Catholic upbringing.

Neither Harvard nor Yale felt right for her.

Then Ken picked her up and took her to his school, the one he spoke of so fondly—Princeton, the fourth oldest college in the United States. Long regarded as one of the finest and most serious-minded of America's colleges and universities, the campus also had an easy vitality that drew Sonia in and made her feel relatively welcome.

The students who greeted Sonia were friendly and engaged. Finally, something clicked. Princeton felt "just right" for Sonia.

PRINCETON OPENS THE DOOR TO KNOWLEDGE

Traditions live long. But the 1970s were a time of change. Accepted into Princeton on a full scholarship, Sonia's class was only the fourth to accept women. Of those women, very few were women of color. Without a "prep" school background, Sonia still felt as though she was in an alien world.

Overwhelmed by her new school and environment, it took a while to get into the groove of college life. New York City was a far cry from Princeton, New Jersey. As a city girl, she could mistake cows for horses. In her early days in her dorm, she kept hearing a chirping sound and couldn't figure out what it was, having never heard a cricket before.

The cultural divide intrigued Sonia more than intimidated her. When her roommate said she was like "Alice," Sonia didn't know who she was referring to. "You don't know who Alice in Wonderland is?" her roommate asked and went on to explain the classic story.

"There was a world I had missed," said Sonia. Hungry to learn more, she asked her roommate for a list of other classics that she might not have read while growing up in a world so far from hers. During the summer after her freshman year, she hit the library and read as many of the classics as she could, including Jane Austen's novels and *Adventures of Huckleberry Finn*, as well as children's books like those that Lewis Carroll had written.

She hadn't lived or experienced what many of her classmates took for granted in their educational or cultural backgrounds. Still an avid reader, it was her pleasure to catch up.

Unprepared for the caliber of competition and educational standards, but with the work ethic her mother had instilled in her, she set out to find resources to help improve her study habits.

Competitive against herself, after her first mid-term paper was returned with low marks, she sought help. "I needed to learn how to write at Princeton," she said.

With every paper, she became better. When she could, she studied grammar books. The chair of the Latin American Studies department guided her. Like other mentors, he wanted to see her succeed. He dissected her writing, circled every noun and adjective, told her to think and write in English rather than try to translate from Spanish to English. Every course she took with him, her writing improved.

It took a while for Sonia to integrate herself and become comfortable in her new surroundings. But she studied them and analyzed them, asking questions to determine which situation best suited her and what all the variables were.

Even getting a poor grade on a mid-term didn't deter her for long. Sonia got to know Princeton, got to know her place in it—and learned how to be an asset to it, as well. Using its resources to further her goal of becoming a judge someday, she started to make her presence known. That dream never left her. In fact, the dream became clearer with every academic success she had.

ACTIVIST ON CAMPUS

The 1970s was a time in United States history when social justice issues were brought to the forefront of Americans' consciousness, especially on college campuses. Students made their voices heard with issues pertaining to civil rights, women's rights, and the United States' participation in the Vietnam War, for example.

Already possessed of a sensitivity for the plight of others, Sonia was able to stay on the path that Senator Robert Kennedy had inspired with his own mission for social justice. She became involved with groups on campus such as Acción Puertorriqueña, a Puerto Rican activist group, and the Third World Center, which provided "a social, cultural and political environment that reflected the needs and concerns of students of color at the University." She found a home at the Third World Center.

Princeton was like living in a parallel world. The Third World Center, however, brought together many different ethnic groups, socio-economic groups, and a diversity of women of color. It was a home to a bigger "family with common interests." This family could better relate to where Sonia came from and what she was about.

She said, "At Princeton, I began a lifelong commitment to identifying myself as a Latina, taking pride in being Hispanic, and in recognizing my obligation to help my community reach its fullest potential in this society. Accion Puertorriqueña, the Puerto Rican group on campus then, and the Third World Center… provided me with the anchor I needed to ground myself in this new and different world."

Not everyone who came from privilege could understand her background. "You have to understand my mother raised us on $5,000 a year," she said.

Some found the groups radical on account of their vehemence in fighting discrimination—protesting, writing letters, meeting with administrators—but it was a platform to improve their conditions and their rights. Sonia saw a bigger world and how decisions could have an impact on not just one person but a ripple effect on communities, states, and even a nation. At the same time, she didn't want to limit herself by surrounding herself exclusively with Latino things. She got all that back home.

Wanting exposure to more, she worked with the university's discipline committee once it was established, and started developing her legal skills. As the student representative on a board made up of faculty and students, she would hear minor cases against students, and help to decide the discipline or punishment.

With her mother and grandmother as role models—healers in their own right—Sonia's work through the Third World Center led her to volunteer as an interpreter at Trenton Psychiatric Hospital. It made her aware of how many people fell through the cracks of the system and were lost.

Between her studies, work, and volunteer efforts, Sonia's energy was at an all-time high. But her diabetes remained an everyday concern. No one really knew her routine included keeping her diabetes in check so that she could live a "normal" life.

Normal included visits from her mother and brother a couple times a year, as well as regular visits from Kevin and a cousin or two. She received weekly correspondence from Abuelita, her lifeline, her connection to those island girl values and all that mattered. But in her sophomore year, when the envelopes didn't arrive for two weeks straight, Sonia asked her mother what was up. And just like that, "normalcy" was shattered.

Abuelita had cancer and was in the hospital. The family had always called Sonia "Mercedes Chiquita"—Little Mercedes— because they were so alike. When Abuelita died, the pain cut into Sonia's heart. Going back to classes, Sonia refocused her energy to make her Abuelita proud of her.

Although she was challenged at first, she pushed herself to really learn, work hard, and serve her communities. All Sonia's hard work paid off when the president of the college called her into his office to tell her the good news: she was graduating with Phi Beta Kappa honors and summa cum laude.

She knew it had to be good, but once again, she didn't know

how good. "I had no idea what summa cum laude meant." As soon as she left his office, she raced to the library to look it up. "With greatest honor," she read.

Sonia's exceptional grades and performance had earned her the highest academic recognition of excellence. This was also reinforced at her 1976 graduation, where she was awarded the Moses Taylor Pyne Honor Prize, the highest academic achievement award given to a Princeton undergraduate. The recipient had to be an "all-rounder"—a student with exceptional character who demonstrated excellence in academics, leadership with campus organizations, and effective support of the best interests of Princeton University.

Sonia more than fit the bill.

Her experiences at Princeton were hugely influential on her later life, and she later described them as "transformative." She had found, in that university, a place of shared values and fierce competition, and made a home for herself there.

Sonia had come to Princeton, an alien land, a castle on the mountaintop, conquered it, and left her mark. But she knew she had much work ahead of her. In her yearbook, next to her photo was a quote from American socialist Norman Thomas, and it read: "I am not a champion of lost causes, but of causes not yet won."

CHAPTER SIX

One Step Closer to a Latina Perry Mason

"I had no need to apologize that the look-wider, search-more affirmative action that Princeton and Yale practiced had opened doors for me. That was its purpose: to create the conditions whereby students from disadvantaged backgrounds could be brought to the starting line of a race many were unaware was even being run."

Shortly after graduating, Sonia married her high school sweetheart, Kevin Noonan, in 1976 at St. Patrick's Cathedral in New York City. Sonia changed her name to Sonia Sotomayor de Noonan. They moved into a small apartment, bought a dog they named Star, and continued their studies. Kevin would eventually become a biologist and patent lawyer.

Meanwhile, Sonia applied to and was admitted to one of the most prestigious law schools in the United States—at Yale University in New Haven, Connecticut. At Yale Law School, the median GPA for applicants was a 3.9, and only 7 percent of applicants were accepted. It was also one of the very first law schools in the nation to admit women. Being Puerto Rican and a woman could have been affirmative action factors that helped Sonia get into Yale, but her stellar Princeton records would have been grounds for acceptance under any circumstances. She received a full ride scholarship, launching her law school venture.

Even though she hadn't felt comfortable on the progressive and activist-heated campus for her undergraduate studies, she was more than ready to get into law after Princeton. It was what she had been dreaming about since she first watched *Perry Mason* on television when she was just ten years old. Ever since those days, she had been mesmerized by the law. This was her chance to make her dream a reality.

In Sonia's first year at Yale, her vision of career and purpose started to gel.

Her M.O.—modus operandi—slipped into gear as she began her usual way of getting used to a new environment, slowly. She assessed her situation, her classes, her professors, her classmates, her surroundings, her shortcomings, and her opportunities. It took well over a year to build her confidence and put herself out there.

She has said that a diverse but close-knit group of four friends in particular—whom she referred to as "brothers"—served as her anchors. They called her "kid" affectionately, and offered her academic and social support. They also challenged her.

It was a throwback to her high school days in the Forensics Club. Some of Sonia's best moments in law school were when she and her classmates sat in a lounge talking and debating the issues of the day. When not in class, other students overbooked their schedules with obligations they thought would look good on their resumes. But the welcome breaks helped Sonia breathe, gave her brain a break, and helped her passions come to the surface. They talked, they debated, and they developed a deepening sense of themselves, their principles, and the law.

Going home to the Bronx always grounded Sonia. Her mother welcomed her friends over and whipped up special Puerto Rican dinners with rice with peas, or pork chops, or just whatever was in the house. It didn't matter. For them it was a safe haven, where they could let loose and talk, discussing the news and class assignments.

Sonia worked as bouncer and bartender at the Graduate and Professional Student Center—GPSC, or better known as the "Gypsy"—where the job was a great social outlet. It also helped pay her expenses while she studied. Outside the classroom, her confidence grew from aligning herself with extracurricular activities, social justice causes, or organizations like LANA, Yale's Latino, Asian, and Native-American student organization.

Sonia sought ways to start making her mark. One way to do that was having a well-researched paper published in the *Yale Law Journal*. The editor at the time, Bill Eskridge, instructed her to bring him a proposal for a possible article. She did. "Statehood and the Equal Footing Doctrine: A Case for Puerto Rican Seabed Rights" was published in 1979.

Before long, Sonia became editor for the *Yale Law Journal* and managing editor of the *Yale Studies in World Public Order*, another publication. Her voice and perspective on controversial issues became stronger. She was not afraid to speak up for the underdog on issues of affirmative action, discrimination, or unfair practices.

In her classes, however, she rarely engaged; that is, until one day, finally, in her third year at Yale Law School, she raised her hand in class. She called out her professor. An equation on the board didn't look right to her. It had to do with the "rules of perpetuity."

These rules determined how far in the future a person could leave property to children and grandchildren. She said his example didn't fit the rule. He studied it, said he'd been teaching it for more than twenty years—and that she was right. He had her come up and teach it!

At Yale, she felt especially vulnerable because the caliber of students created stiff competition. But years of living as an outsider helped her assess people and situations. Her ability to study an issue, analyze it, and ask questions if she didn't understand it, helped with her studies and in her legal career.

Once she got started with a line of questioning, she was like a sponge—she wanted to understand all sides of an issue. Her friends tested her. They tried to compliment her and said she argued like a guy. At first she was offended by the remark, but when they explained, she understood their perspective.

Even though the Women's Movement was going strong during those years, in the classrooms at Yale and other educational institutions, women traditionally didn't speak up. In the classroom, her friends said, female students raised their hands timidly, almost apologetically, to ask a question. But Sonia didn't. Once she built up the courage to ask a question, she was straightforward and direct. No one would ever think she was shy or self-conscious, but it took great effort to shed the protective, self-defensive layers that kept people from seeing the core of her being.

"I had some measure of self-confidence but not enough to feel secure among my very brilliant Yale classmates," she said. "I spent a whole lot of time in law school feeling inadequate and not quite sure I measured up to the accomplishments of my classmates."

Her confidence grew, however, outside the classroom. When she practiced mock trials in a courtroom, she felt right at home. Working alongside attorney mentors who worked for civil rights fueled her passion for serving her community. In mock trial competitions—the Thomas Swan Barristers' Union competition in particular—Sonia felt for the first time that she could be an actual lawyer.

All her knowledge, Latino upbringing, class and work experience, and extracurricular activities like speech and debate competitions (along with watching her abuela enchant audiences with her poetry readings) seemed to click. It was like putting together the ultimate performance. Her job was to convince the audience, the jury, that what she said was truth.

She prepared well. She tried to read body language. She used her hands to gesture and emphasize a point or two. The cadence of her voice rose and fell depending on the information she tried to relay. The feedback she received from the jury members helped her learn her strengths and weaknesses.

Working with mentors like José Cabranes, who had founded the Puerto Rican Legal Defense and Education Fund, also made her grow. He had served as counsel to the governor of Puerto Rico and was general counsel to Yale while Sonia was in law school. Charlie Hey-Maestre, a Princeton classmate, came to meet with him to work on his thesis and told Sonia all about him and his work in civil rights for Hispanics, a cause close to her heart. Sonia realized Cabranes was more than a professor. He was an actual attorney who was making a difference, doing what she aspired to do. When Charlie introduced them, Sonia was hooked by his knowledge and passion, and their discussions made her think critically of real-life issues affecting individuals in communities across the nation. After a three-hour lunch, Cabranes asked her to come work for him during the summer.

Sonia didn't hesitate. She did research for the book he was writing on U.S. citizenship and Puerto Ricans, and assisted with minor legal work for the university. She learned mostly from shadowing Cabranes—the way he interacted with different groups of people, his passion for the law, and his seeming genuine interest in getting to know a person or issue behind a case.

When graduation time neared, students interviewed with potential law firms. Besides excelling in her classes, Sonia had been involved with activist groups, had worked real jobs, and had actual experience working with real attorneys. Her resume was impressive and she was ready for interviews.

One night, Sonia sat at a dinner table with a representative from the law firm Shaw, Pittman, Potts & Trowbridge and other law students. The firm liked to hire from Yale because of the caliber of graduate. However, without looking at Sonia's resume or work and volunteer history, one the firm's partners, Martin Krall, asked questions about affirmative action that Sonia thought were discriminatory.

He insinuated that the only reason she was admitted to Yale was because of affirmative action. He asked whether law firms did a disservice by hiring underqualified minority students with inferior credentials who couldn't compete in the real world of lawyering—and then firing them a few years later.

His rudeness and assumption shocked Sonia. She did not make a scene that night, but she could not let his remarks go. "I thought it presumptuous and racist, quite frankly," she said.

If he had checked her records, he would have seen that she graduated summa cum laude and with the Pyne Award from Princeton, and had achieved high standards of excellence in other areas of her academic and professional life. Being an affirmative action recipient had only allowed her the opportunity to get into colleges like Princeton and Yale. The rest—challenging herself to excel and surpass standards of excellence—had been up to her. It was as if she had to work doubly hard to prove herself and compete.

The next day she decided to hold him accountable and stand up to his racially insensitive remarks, starting with his impression of affirmative action.

First she told him that she'd been taught manners by her mother—and that included not making others uncomfortable. Then she explained that affirmative action gave kids like her opportunity where there had been none before. His remarks were insulting and his judgment of her and her capabilities and achievements was unfair. She was one of those kids who had made the most of her opportunity.

Sonia then filed a formal complaint against the recruiter for violating Yale's antidiscrimination policy. It was a risky move because the firm had recruited from Yale grads for years and it could deteriorate the relationship between the firm and the university. But for Sonia, it was the right thing to do.

A Yale student-faculty tribunal ruled in her favor and ordered the firm to issue an apology or risk being banned from on-campus recruitment of Yale Law School students.

News of the incident spread across the nation. Other minority groups and organizations started speaking up about similar offensive remarks and experiences they had faced. It seemed like an antidiscrimination rally was fueled, and affirmative action recipients didn't have to remain silent to derogatory remarks aimed at their integrity or capabilities.

Shaw, Pittman, Potts & Trowbridge issued a full and public apology. The story was picked up by the *Washington Post*. Sonia was relieved that she was not blacklisted from other law firms. That meant that she was still considered a good candidate to hire. Even then her career took a different turn from what she ever expected.

One evening when she was studying late on campus, she walked down a hallway in the library, and a panel on "Public Service Career Paths" was taking place in a conference room. Intrigued, she slowed down. The perk? Free food was offered. She decided to stay, if only to grab some cheddar cheese at the end of the spiel.

The panelists spoke about public interest service and how students should give that a try versus private practice. New York District Attorney Robert Morgenthau sounded convincing. Suddenly, the idea of being in a courtroom straight out of college with her own criminal cases, rather than shadowing senior partners for years before being handed a case, sounded like just what Sonia needed to jumpstart her career.

In a *Perry Mason* episode she saw as a girl, Hamilton Burger, the DA who lost every week, still impressed her. He said he was proud of doing the right thing when the guilty were convicted and the innocent set free.

That belief made Sonia interested in becoming a district attorney. Morgenthau's job stirred a memory of what had first intrigued her about being a lawyer: the chance to seek justice in a courtroom. His offer resonated with her. "You may have your career all planned out, but when a chance comes, you have to be flexible enough to jump," Sonia said.

Her friends thought it was the kiss of death for her career. She wouldn't make much money. Yale Law students were supposed to aspire to private practice, clerkships, or pro bono—free—clinics with prison disciplinary hearings or veterans' benefits. After asking Morgenthau questions about his career and the opportunities, her gut told her to take a leap of faith when he invited her to visit his offices in New York.

In 1979, Sonia earned her Juris Doctorate—JD—from Yale Law School. After she passed the bar in 1980, she immediately began work as a rookie assistant district attorney in New York.

All her textbooks, lessons, mock trials, and extracurricular work at Yale Law School only touched the tip of the iceberg for criminal law. Nothing prepared her for facing real-life criminal cases in real-life court. This was the first step in becoming the Latina Perry Mason in the court of law.

CHAPTER SEVEN

Seeking Justice for All in the Courtroom

"We educated, privileged lawyers have a professional and moral duty to represent the underrepresented in our society, to ensure that justice exists for all, both legal and economic justice."

Sonia's move—leaving for the streets of New York to work with the District Attorney's office—shocked professors and friends. Most Yale graduates could get their pick of job offers, even if they started at entry-level positions of large prestigious firms. Sonia wanted to try cases, stand before a jury, and plead a case. When she accepted DA Morgenthau's offer to work for his office as an assistant, she knew she would get her days in court.

NEW YORK DISTRICT ATTORNEY'S OFFICE

In the offices, Sonia and the thirty-nine other first-year associates were known as "ducklings." They followed Morgenthau and the experienced attorneys, trying to keep up. Criminal case training didn't happen in the classroom. This was no longer playacting in mock trials or watching *Perry Mason* on television.

Serving as a prosecutor in the courtroom meant Sonia's job was to protect the public. From 1979 to 1984, she was responsible for prosecuting robbery, assault, murder, police brutality, and child pornography cases. In 1979 there was a crime wave in New York and also budget cuts that affected law enforcement agencies, so there were fewer police officers on the streets to deal with the crimes being committed. The mayor at the time, Ed Koch, promised to "restore order."

The DA's office was busy as the pile of cases grew, but Sonia was a fast learner. Working fifteen-hour days, she did a lot of legwork on her own to build her cases. That way she got to know the neighborhoods and the people. She made it a point to hear different perspectives of a story and search for details that others might miss. She asked many questions to get to the truth as best she could understand it. Determined to be fair, she listened.

Understanding and respecting the law is the job of an attorney, but there were so many layers in every case. Sonia believed police and prosecutors needed to be more sensitive to potential unfair racial and gender disparities in the system. She saw people make honest mistakes in identifying alleged suspects incorrectly, those they thought "might" be guilty. A mistake landed innocent people in jail and changed the course of their lives forever. Then there were people who committed a crime—like a petty theft—but perhaps they were mentally ill.

As the years rolled on, and as Sonia improved at her job, it still took a toll on her inherent optimism. She was becoming hard and cynical. It was a side effect of her job. She understood that her role as a prosecutor served a specific purpose in the justice system.

With Morgenthau's urging and support, Sonia also became a board member of the Puerto Rican Legal Defense and Education Fund. PRLDEF ("Pearl-def") challenged discrimination cases against the Hispanic community. It was a way to keep her happy and proud of social justice cases across the nation that went right.

Still, the cases before the DA's office were dismal and depressing.

One of the most notorious cases she assisted in the prosecution of was the "Tarzan Murderer." The accused was a burglar, but unlike other burglars, he stood out for his athleticism. Like a trapeze artist, he swung on ropes, down from rooftops, from apartment to apartment and window to window. He'd swing into the apartments and shoot and rob victims, sometimes killing them, and then swing out again. He would be identified for this "skill" because not many people could perform it. It took a lot of upper body strength and agility.

Sonia and her team gathered evidence against him once they had him in custody. In interviewing the victims, witnesses and survivors of loved ones who had been killed, Sonia saw the ripple effect of devastation.

During the course of the trial, she looked into the eyes of the Tarzan Murderer for some sign of remorse. Anything. There was nothing. She learned—and believed, for the first time in her life—how some human beings might actually be inherently irredeemable. It began to warp her thought of humanity.

The Tarzan Murderer was sentenced to sixty-seven-and-a-half years in prison.

The case took a toll on her. After that, Sonia knew her days at the DA's office were numbered. Even though in one of her job evaluations she was described as a "potential superstar," in 1984 she left to start working for private practice.

THE LAW TAKES A TOLL AT HOME

The three worlds of study, work, and marriage started to separate for Sonia. The daily grind and strenuous hours took a toll. Her husband, Kevin, also realized that no matter how hard he worked, he might not ever be as successful as her. Being so independent, she would never need him. They didn't see that as a negative factor, just as a natural fact of their relationship and who they were as individuals.

Sonia said, "I loved him and I knew he loved me, but did I need him the way he needed me to? No. We were the best of friends. But it wasn't fair to him or to me."

Sonia knew marriage was about compromise—and that it was okay when marriages failed. Some women believed they "could have it all"—careers and marriages, giving 100 percent to both. After trying that, she leaned more toward the belief of needing to live a life that asks "What makes you happy?" rather than "Can you have it all?"

In 1983, Kevin and Sonia amicably divorced. They would each go on to find happiness and fulfillment on their own terms, in their own careers.

Sonia remained single. They did not have children. Although she sometimes thought about that decision, the choice was one she elected not to take. Her role as a godmother to several children gave her fulfillment in that area of her life.

PRIVATE PRACTICE OFFERS ANOTHER PERSPECTIVE OF THE LAW

For a while, after leaving the DA's office, Sotomayor opened a solo practice, which she operated out of her apartment in Brooklyn. In 1984, she joined the private practice Pavia and Harcourt as a civil litigator. Based in New York, the firm had only thirty lawyers. Cases focused on copyright infringement and intellectual property laws, real estate, counterfeiting, and warranty disputes. Clients included international corporations like Ferrari, Bulgari, and Fendi, fashion designers who wanted to take vendors to court for making "knock-offs" of their exclusive, expensive Italian handbags and selling them for a fraction of the cost.

At Pavia and Harcourt, Sonia found more mentors in George Pavia, the Jewish refugee founder's son; Dave Botwinik, the partner who was the go-to for any question on ethics; and Fran Bernstein, who became a friend and female ally. Sonia learned about collaborative, transparent sharing of sources and developing an environment that was comfortable and personable, but where the team got the job done for its clients.

No matter what kind of cases Sonia was representing, she still found law fascinating. "In the practice of law, there are rules that establish a minimum standard of acceptable conduct: what the law permits." Those were guidelines, standards, and rules that were the law of the land—that all Americans should follow unless there were some extenuating circumstances that could prove otherwise.

When Pavia and Harcourt hired her, she promised she would stay with them for as long as she remained in private practice. Botwinik asked that she stay at least until she was tapped to become a Supreme Court Justice. At first, she thought he was joking, but he wasn't. It was the first time anyone in her field had ever seen the deepest secret in her heart, had ever believed she had the capability to get there. When she became a partner after Fran's death, it was bittersweet. She wanted to make her proud.

The promise made her push herself even more. Besides her work in the office, she began to take on a bigger role in the community and make a difference at another level in public service. Sonia was appointed by Governor Mario Cuomo to the State of New York Mortgage Agency and served until 1992. Mayor Ed Koch also appointed her to the New York City Campaign Finance Board and to the Board of Directors of the Puerto Rican Legal Defense and Education Fund.

Sonia learned another valuable thing: being more open about herself showed her who her true her friends were. All along her career journey, she'd kept her diabetes secret. She did not want to show weakness or vulnerability. They didn't even know about it until she started fading at parties and at work.

It was at her thirty-seventh birthday when Sonia hit a sugar low and had to ask for help. The card she'd written and kept close but hidden had to be pulled out of her wallet. It read:

I HAVE DIABETES

I am not drunk. If I am unconscious or acting strangely, I may have low blood sugar.

EMERGENCY TREATMENT

I need sugar immediately…

After that, she never kept her disease a secret again. Being open about it helped others who suffered from it, especially children, to not feel ashamed and stay strong in difficult circumstances.

She was able to go about her work and still continue on her career path. The doors to the courtroom were about to burst open for Sonia. Her friend and mentor Dave Botwinik's words about the Supreme Court rained down over her like a blessing. It would start to become a reality sooner than she ever imagined.

CHAPTER EIGHT

Slipping into the Black Robes

"Judges can't rely on what's in their heart. They don't determine the law. Congress makes the law. The job of a judge is to apply the law."

One day, after a long-deserved Christmas break, Sonia returned to Pavia and Harcourt to find her desk cleared off—except for one sheet of paper. It was an application form for a federal district court judge position.

To apply to be a judge was a big move for Sonia. Federal and appellate judges go through a long evaluation process and, if selected to move on through various levels of interviews, can only be appointed by the President of the United States—with approval by the U.S. Senate.

There are three branches of the United States government. The executive is made up of the president and vice-president. The legislative branch is made up of Congress, which includes the Senate and House of Representatives. The judicial branch is made up of the Supreme Court at the highest level, followed by ninety-four federal district courts spread across the country and thirteen circuit courts of appeals within those districts.

Federal courts deal with the U.S. Constitution and laws passed by Congress that can affect the nation. State courts are established by a state and although they enforce federal laws, their courts are specific to that state.

In Federal district courts, civil and criminal cases are both tried, but civil cases predominate. Defendants in that particular district are tried, witnesses testify, and juries serve. The decision made in the trial can affect the mass population of the country. Civil cases can include cases that affect things like a person's rights in the workplace. For example, a case can be about a company that refused to hire a person simply because she was a woman, or an employer that refused to pay social security benefits to a former employee.

If the defendant loses, he might be ordered to pay money to the plaintiff. These cases might help change laws about hiring rights or give guidelines for future similar cases.

A defendant also has the right to take his case to a court of appeals if he loses.

Sonia was very aware of the chain of command, having been in many courtrooms in her young life. But she had been facing the judge in all those cases she had presented. To see the application on her desk was scary. It was her next career move. Her dream. And she was being called out to act on it.

Botwinik explained that New York's Democratic Senator Daniel Patrick Moynihan was on the Judicial Selection Committee for the federal district court position. He would sift through a list of potential candidates before making its recommendation to the President of the United States, George H.W. Bush. Her pro bono work had also caught the attention of Senator Edward Kennedy. She was on the radar with the politicians who could forward her career to a judgeship.

Botwinik told her to fill out the application.

She responded, "Are you crazy? I'm thirty-six years old!"

He told her they were looking for qualified Hispanics and that she was "…eminently qualified. Period."

His support and belief in her boggled her mind. It took her a week to fill out the incredibly lengthy application. The nomination process was intense and took eighteen months, but Senator Moynihan ended up recommending her. The support from the community, colleagues, and the public was overwhelming. Her career received a big boost when, in 1991, she was nominated, at the age of 36, by President Bush to the judgeship on the U.S. District Court for the Southern District of New York. The U.S. Senate unanimously confirmed her on August 11, 1992.

Her title was District Judge Sotomayor. She was the youngest and the first Hispanic in the state's history to serve as a federal judge. She was also the first Puerto Rican woman to serve as a federal judge. She moved back to the Bronx to live in her district.

One of her first official acts as a judge was marrying her mother Celina to her long-time boyfriend, Omar Lopez. It seemed almost fitting that she returned to her roots, her neighborhood, and sealed a special relationship. The acts might have reminded her to stay grounded as she stepped onto the bench as a trial judge.

The dreams she had as a girl, watching *Perry Mason*, were coming true. Making the transition to being a judge had been her long-term goal when she was first diagnosed with diabetes and couldn't pursue a career as a detective.

Now addressed as Judge Sotomayor in her courtroom, Sonia had to address the law in a different way. Her first year as a district court judge was one of the most difficult times in her life as she adjusted to being on the other side of the bench. Her judicial philosophy started to develop over time as she worked her way up through the system, observed the different approaches of her colleagues, and learned more and more about the law in general.

Sonia asked tough questions of the attorneys presenting their cases. Unprepared attorneys were taken to task. She wanted to make sure she understood all the facts before making her determination. This practice followed her every step of her career. "When I ask tough questions on the bench—lawyers understand this—it's because I'm grappling with a tough issue. It's not an attempt to embarrass the lawyer; it's to ensure the lawyer has given me the best answer to help me understand."

In her role as a U.S. District Court Judge, Sonia became known as "the judge who saved baseball."

In 1994, for more than seven months, Major League Baseball (MLB) players went on strike because the owners were stalling on negotiations regarding, mostly, salary issues. The strike cut the 1994 season short, including playoffs and the World Series. By January 1995, the federal government got involved, introducing bills in Congress that would put a stop to it. It didn't work. President Clinton ordered the players and owners to reach an agreement by February 6. It didn't happen. The baseball owners decided they would bring in replacement players—and the National Labor Relations Board (NLRB) filed an "unfair labor practices complaint" against them.

The case came before Sonia. She did her homework. After almost a year of negotiations, and with the 1995 National baseball season at risk from starting on time, the MLB strike had become the longest work stoppage in professional sports history. She had a lot of reading to do. A die-hard baseball fan, she knew the game. She asked hard questions of both sides—owners, and players' representatives in court—but told them she didn't want to hear witnesses or read any more documents.

In March, she issued an injunction. An injunction is a last resort court order used in special cases that stops a person or company from continuing an action that threatens or invades the legal rights of others; it can prevent a possible injustice from happening.

The injunction Sonia issued meant neither side won. It ordered the MLB owners to stop what they were doing—they could not make their own rules about labor relations and player contracts—and let the baseball season get underway. The injunction was like they were given a time out. They could take a deep breath, regroup, and restore the terms of the previous year's labor agreement, just so they could play ball as regularly scheduled. Her decision was upheld by the Supreme Court.

The players came back for opening day that April. The baseball strike was over long enough to get the season going and get America's favorite pasttime back on its feet. The fans were ready. The media played up Sonia's part in ending the strike.

Every case Sonia took on, she tackled the same way, whether it received media attention or not. She stayed on the radar of Washington, D.C., and her trek toward the Supreme Court suddenly didn't seem like such a crazy idea.

On June 25, 1997, President Clinton nominated Judge Sotomayor to a seat on the U.S. Court of Appeals for the Second Circuit. Confirmation came with a 67-39 vote on October 2, 1998.

She remained on the Second Circuit for ten years and heard more than three thousand cases. Her rulings including upholding the National Football League's (NFL) eligibility rules requiring players to wait three full seasons after high school graduation before entering the NFL draft.

In her time on the bench, there was one thing that never wavered—her belief in the law. "I am and have always been a rule follower," she said. "But there's something about judging that required a certain type of vision, not seeing beyond the case or policy, but to see the entire relationship of those cases to the law."

She not only applied the law, but she began to teach law, too. Sonia became an adjunct law professor at New York University and then at Columbia Law School. At this time, she also became a member of the Second Circuit Task Force on Gender, Racial, and Ethnic Fairness in the Courts. This task force worked to prevent discrimination in the courts and issued reports after questioning attorneys, judges, and others working in the court system.

As a Second Circuit judge, some of Sonia's cases were overruled by the Supreme Court. Her interaction with the Supreme Court was just beginning. Soon she would see the other side of the highest court of the land.

CHAPTER NINE

Sonia Style: Making Her Way to the Supreme Court

"I think that the day a justice forgets that each decision comes at a cost to someone, then I think you start losing your humanity."

The path to becoming a judge took hard work. Even though it was a time in American history that was changing in civil rights for women and minorities, Sonia still experienced discrimination. Sometimes men in the courtroom treated her dismissively—until they realized she was the judge and gave the ultimate last word in a case decision. The wisdom to be a judge grew with experience—not only in the courtroom, but in life experience.

Sonia knew how demoralizing it could be for women in the courtroom to keep seeing men put woman down. That was as true for attorneys as it was for any public servant. "You have to recognize it, accept it for what it is and push past it," she said.

She pushed past it by being strong in voice and intention—and not backing down. "That's just who I am. I have a style that is Sonia, and it is more assertive than many women are, or even some men. There's nothing wrong with being a little bit quieter than me or more timid than me, but if you're doing it all of the time and not waiting for the moments where you need to be more assertive and take greater control, then you won't be successful."

She also knew how to tone it down at the right moments. The style that was Sonia worked for her as a judge. It put the law first. It placed the belief in equal justice for all at the forefront. It didn't compromise her individuality. Wearing bright red nail polish and lipstick, and occasionally animal print high heels, she stood out as unique and individualistic. Yet, she represented a growing U.S. Hispanic population—being able to speak Spanish as well as English.

President George H.W. Bush saw that in her. President Bill Clinton saw that in her. In 2009, President Barack Obama saw that in her.

The Supreme Court of the United States, the highest court of the land, has room for nine sitting justices. (A justice is the term used instead of judge.) When Justice David Souter retired in 2009, Sonia's name was given to President Obama on a short list of nominees as the possible replacement. President Obama sought a justice with a "common touch" and empathy—someone who could relate well to others.

When President Obama called to tell Sonia he had nominated her, she realized how big a deal it was, that the nomination was bigger than anything she'd ever dreamed possible for herself. She held her hand over her heart, sure that he could hear how loudly it beat in excitement.

On May 26, 2009, President Obama announced her nomination to the Supreme Court. Citing her accomplishments, he introduced her, saying, "I've decided to nominate an inspiring woman who I believe will make a great justice." He congratulated her without hesitation.

It turned into a whirlwind experience for Sonia.

The process was intense. Sonia was grilled for months. At one point during this process, she was running through the La Guardia airport in New York to catch a flight to Washington, D.C., for more interviews, when she stumbled and broke her ankle. She initially refused treatment, but by the end of the day, she saw a doctor and was put in a cast and on crutches. It didn't slow her down much. She met with all her interviewers, lobbied for herself, and hustled from meeting to meeting and office to office until she was finished for the day.

Every aspect of her life was put under a microscope—from cases she had ruled on to things she had said to parts of her life that were private. She answered truthfully and to the best to her ability. In July, 2009, for four consecutive days at a Senate hearing, people testified for and against her nomination. She listened to every person, every comment. And then…

The Senate confirmed her on August 6, 2009, on a 68-31 vote. Seventy-four days after her nomination, Sonia started working as a justice.

Hispanics celebrated her appointment to the Supreme Court as a first—the first Latina and first woman of color to hold the position. Family, friends, colleagues, and supporters from the Bronx saw one of their own make it. From Mayagüez, Puerto Rico, to Los Angeles, California—all across the nation, it seemed—people were waiting for someone like Sonia, someone like them, to reach this pinnacle of success. Sonia made them proud. Her life as a Justice would have a great impact inside and outside the Supreme Court Building.

CHAPTER TEN

The People's Justice

*"If you love law the way I do... you're given the job
of a lifetime... you're permitted to address the most
important legal questions of the country, and sometimes
the world. And in doing so, you make a difference in
people's lives."*

On August 8, 2009, the day dawned like any other in Washington, D.C. Where Sonia Sotomayor was concerned, however, the day was like no other, feeling almost like a fairy tale where dreams come true. It started as a "day of firsts."

Sonia was to become the first Hispanic justice in the Supreme Court's history. She would be the first woman of color to sit on the Supreme Court.

Where she was sworn in was symbolic, too. For the first time, a justice would be sworn in at a formal conference room at the Supreme Court Building instead of at the White House. And for the first time, cameras were allowed in to record the event.

President Obama believed swearing-in ceremonies for justices at the White House in previous years sent the wrong signal. It could have given the impression that the justice was beholden to the president or would owe a favor. The president thought a break with seven decades of tradition would show that her work would not be influenced by the executive or legislative branch of the government.

A show of independence between the White House and the Supreme Court started with the swearing in of Sonia Sotomayor. The Supreme Court Building was the perfect place for the swearing in ceremony.

THE MAJESTY OF THE
SUPREME COURT BUILDING

Created in 1789, the Supreme Court is the "court of last resort" in the United States. The Supreme Court Building stands in the heart of Washington, D. C., across from the state capitol, regal in its role—the sacred place where the law is decided and the national ideal of justice is served.

"The Republic endures and this is the symbol of its faith." Chief Justice Charles Evans Hughes spoke these words when breaking ground for the Supreme Court Building on October 13, 1932. The building symbolized the importance and connection of the Supreme Court and the American judicial system.

A few low steps lead up to the 252-foot-wide oval plaza in front of the building. On either side of the main steps sit large marble statues by sculptor James Earle Fraser. On the left is the female *Contemplation of Justice*. On the right is the male *Guardian of Law*. *Justice* holds sword and scales, and *The Three Fates* weave the thread of life.

Bronze flagpole bases are crested with symbolic designs of the scales and sword, the book, the mask and torch, the pen and mace, and the four elements: air, earth, fire, and water.

Sixteen marble columns lead up to the main west entrance. The inscription above it reads: "Equal Justice Under Law." Just above the engraving is a Robert Aitken sculpture of the crowned Lady Liberty seated on a throne, flanked by figures on either side of her who symbolically represent Order and Authority. They are there to protect and to guard her.

On the back, or east entrance of the building, "Justice the Guardian of Liberty," is engraved, with figures of famous lawmakers, like Moses and Confucius, carved above it.

The monumental bronze doors at the top of the front steps weigh more than six tons each and open into the main corridor, known as the Great Hall. Busts of all former chief justices are prominently displayed along the side walls.

At the east end of the Great Hall, oak doors open into the court chamber. Twenty-four marble columns lead into the main chamber. The raised mahogany bench where the justices sit during sessions was redesigned in 1972 into a "winged" shape. It provides better sight and sound advantages over the original straight design.

At the left of the bench sits the clerk. Responsible for administering the court dockets and argument calendars, the clerk supervises the admission of attorneys to the Supreme Court Bar. To the right of the bench sits the marshal. As the timekeeper of Court sessions, the marshal signals with white and red lights how much time a lawyer has left.

The attorneys arguing cases before the Court position themselves at the tables in front of the bench. When it is their turn to argue, they address the bench from the lectern in the center. Guests, dignitaries, officers of the court, the press, and the public are designated to specific seating areas.

For Sonia, who had first fallen in love with the law as a result of reading *Nancy Drew* novels and watching *Perry Mason* on television, perhaps looking up past those columns into that engraving "Equal Justice Under All," the reality was a bit overwhelming. What a journey it had been to make it here.

But maybe the power had always been within her. She'd made it to her new home, to where she was meant to be all along.

THE OATH FOREVER

In what is called the investiture process—the swearing in of a new justice—Sonia was at once elated and overcome with what the moment meant, not only to her, but what it represented to the Hispanic population. The magnitude of the moment didn't escape her. Not one to cry easily, tears escaped her.

Sonia walked with pride into the conference room, without the need for crutches. Her ankle had completely healed in the time it had taken to go through the long confirmation and interview process. Chief Justice John Roberts cited the oath, and Sonia repeated the solemn words:

> "I, Sonia Sotomayor, do solemnly swear that I will administer justice without respect to persons, and do equal right without respect to persons, and do equal right to the poor and to the rich, and that

I will faithfully and impartially discharge and perform all the duties incumbent upon me as the Associate Justice of the Supreme Court of the United States under the Constitution and laws of the United States. So help me God."

Hugs from her mother and brother, smiles, handshakes and well-wishes from those in the audience overwhelmed her. She beamed. After a few minutes, she and Chief Justice Roberts made their way to the front of the Supreme Court Building. Standing in front of the majestic white columns with Lady Liberty looking down upon them, the newest addition to the Supreme Court, Justice Sonia Sotomayor, faced the throng of reporters.

Her moment in the spotlight revolved around her being the first Hispanic justice and only the third female justice in the history of the Supreme Court.

A SUPREME COURT JUSTICE DUTIES

The first case Sonia heard as a Supreme Court justice was *Citizens United v. Federal Election Commission*, where she dissented from the majority. This case had to do with the rights of corporations in campaign finance. In other early cases on the bench, Sonia went on to vote in favor of protection of affirmative action programs, and she ruled to uphold the Affordable Care Act and to legalize same-sex marriage (in *Obergefell v. Hodges)*.

Justices have other responsibilities besides hearing and deciding cases. Each justice is assigned to one of thirteen federal circuits and can oversee emergency decisions such as setting bond for a defendant, stopping the deportation of an undocumented immigrant, or act on a stay of execution. Since they are also representatives of the United States, justices can also educate the public by meeting with writers, heads of state, and other people in the cultural spotlight.

They also read a lot. "Reading is the life of a justice," Sonia said. They read briefs, prior Supreme Court cases, and opinions. The justices meet every Friday for conferences to discuss cases and their positions on an issue. The meetings start with Chief Justice John Roberts and are then followed by the other justices in order of seniority. Sonia said she uses the same skills she used as a lawyer to try to persuade others to join her and see things from her perspective.

> "When the Supreme Court takes a case, it's because there is a disagreement among the courts below. It means that the issues are not clear under existing law. All of that lack of clarity is usually around issues that are important to the society—like Obamacare, same-sex marriage—and every decision we make is final. Every time we decide, even when I'm in the majority and I think we're right, you know that there's a loser. There is another side who is going to feel something negative about what has happened. And that makes this job harder.
>
> Once we decide, there is no more hope."

THE PROCESS

When the Court starts a public session, the justices are announced by the marshal. When the gavel sounds, those in attendance stand. Then the robed justices sit. The traditional chant rings out:

> The Honorable, the Chief Justice and the Associate Justices of the Supreme Court of the United States. Oyez! Oyez! Oyez! All persons having business before the Honorable, the Supreme Court of the United States, are admonished to draw near and give their attention, for the Court is now sitting. God save the United States and this Honorable Court!

Court is in session from October through June and then breaks for summer, although it seems a justice's work is never done. They usually spend the summers going over cases in their offices with their clerks and writing opinions. Approximately ten thousand petitions are filed with the Court each year, and the justices must decide which will make it to the top of the recommendation list when they resume in October again. The Rule of Four governs their choices: if four justices vote to hear a case, then all the justices agree to it.

They do try to hear cases that can impact the masses rather than just the two parties appearing in court. An example is a case where a student sues an assistant principal for searching a locker. This might become an issue of privacy rights of all students in public schools.

Despite the strong disagreements that might arise over cases, the justices usually respect each other's intellect and good faith. Former Justice John Paul Stevens was Sonia's closest confidante her first year. His patience in offering guidance about the law and judicial process helped her confidence grow.

WHAT SONIA PRACTICES IN THE COURTROOM

Justice Sotomayor slipped into her black robes without skipping a beat, looking as if she has always meant to be a part of the Supreme Court. Her practices remain the same as in her other judgeships. She calls herself a "citizen lawyer." She asks a lot of questions, analyzes the material, researches on her own, and has little respect for unprepared attorneys.

Known for her kindness toward jurors and the attorneys who work hard to advocate for their clients, she holds high standards. Her values that led her to the Supreme Court grounds her in her decision-making. She still works long hours and expects the same from her clerks.

While she was not a religious fanatic, she did go back to her roots, and the Catholic in her often emerges in the way she acts or the values she deems important. A mantra she uses for empowerment in her job is: "Oh, my God, help me!" And she means it.

Her decisions often argue for granting greater protection to the underrepresented members of society. She respects her colleagues and tries to get along with all of them, even the ones she usually disagrees with, because they are "going to be there for a long time." Even with their differences, she knows they can reach conclusions that will serve the greater good.

Nicknamed "The Lone Dissenter," she is not afraid of being the only justice to stand on one side of a case while all other justices rule on the opposite side of the case. She also writes out her opinions to explain her decisions.

Sometimes, even as days pass and her experience on the Supreme Court grows, Sonia can clearly see the great divide of where she has come from—her background and struggles—compared to the other justices. That difference did not have to be a negative factor in her personal or professional life.

"When you move from one world to the next, you can sometimes feel alienated from them all. The thing I do that helps me is to try to hold on to the positive of every world I'm in," she said. All her worlds overlap with the common elements of emotion, like love and caring, shared experiences, and memories. "As long as I keep focused on that and less on the differences, then I find myself staying connected."

Seeing each colleague as an individual helps Sonia respect their decision-making process with every case.

A LIFETIME COMMITMENT

Seen as one of the most powerful Latinas in the United States, Sonia enjoys her work as a justice, but she never realized how difficult it would be. When she was a district and appellate judge, she took some comfort in knowing that closed cases would reach the Supreme Court for final decisions. Now that she is on the side of the bench where final decisions can impact the masses, she feels the responsibility.

The Constitution states that justices "shall hold their Offices during good Behaviour." This means a Supreme Court justice's term ends only when they retire or from death—or they can only be removed from office by impeachment.

In every position she has been in, there were those who didn't think she was qualified or could do the work. She proved them wrong.

Sonia knew how lucky she was as she walked side by side with President Obama and Vice President Joe Biden, down the halls of the White House, toward the dream she'd had since she was ten years old. She also knew she had worked hard to get there. To walk up the grand, expansive staircase of the Supreme Court Building, to honor the law of the land and try her best to do right by the American people.

Even though some decisions can be controversial, nervewracking, or heartrending, over the years she learned to trust herself and her decisions.

CHAPTER ELEVEN

The Rock Star Life

"I realized that people had an unreal image of me, that somehow I was a god on Mount Olympus. I decided that if I were going to make use of my role as a Supreme Court Justice, it would be to inspire people to realize that, first, I was just like them and second, if I could do it, so could they."

Since being tapped by President Obama to serve as the twenty-ninth Supreme Court justice, the first Latina Supreme Court justice, and the third female justice, Sonia's life has been in the spotlight. She came to the U.S. Supreme Court with more federal judicial experience than any justice in a hundred years, and with more overall judicial experience than anyone in seventy years. She was a superstar.

Her time spent as an assistant district attorney, Court of Appeals and district court judge in New York gave her some of that experience.

This was quite the accomplishment for someone who had been questioned as to how she could possibly have scored higher than her classmates in standardized tests, how she could possibly have gotten into Princeton in the first place. How an affirmative action baby took advantage of the opportunities that opened for her—but worked her butt off to graduate at the top of her class and become what many in American political arenas would call the most powerful Latina in the United States. She spoke her mind, seeking social justice for issues and people who needed defending even when it was not always the popular choice.

Once she became a justice, people began treating Sonia like she was a rock star. Or a god on Mount Olympus. It was the first time a Supreme Court justice had quite the following that Sonia had. A charmed life, it appeared, to all who witnessed from the glass doors looking in. When news reporter Maria Hinojosa of Latino USA on NPR asked how her happy childhood influenced her success, Sonia looked at her and knew she had to set the record straight. Her childhood had often been far from happy.

The idea to write her story—*My Beloved World*—was born. She became a true people's justice for telling her life story of trials and tribulations and overcoming challenges, while also always moving toward her goal of becoming a judge.

"That was the reason I wanted to write the book. So people could see it wasn't easy, that I had to work hard, that if I could make it, a little girl with struggling parents, an alcoholic father, a bilingual background, poverty, and less than perfect surroundings, then they too could aspire to do something with their lives."

A book deal with Knopf Doubleday earned Sonia a seven-figure advance, reportedly $1.2 million. Modeling her memoir after President Obama's *Dreams from My Father*, she had the assistance of poet Zara Houshmand to get the story just so.

Published simultaneously in English and Spanish, *My Beloved World* made the *New York Times* bestseller list. It won praise for its emotional pull. Its success grew and grew.

The speaking engagements began. The crowds gathered. The paparazzi followed. And the spotlight cast its beam on Sonia's rise from a South Bronx housing project to the nation's highest court. Even though the book told of her hardships, it was also like a love letter to her life growing up in the Bronx.

Like the latest rock star or reality TV celebrity, when Sonia makes appearances, thousands of people show up to hear what she has to say—about law, her life, women's rights, human rights, education, diversity, and opportunity. People saw the glamor and glitz. They saw the likes on social media and her millions of followers on Twitter and Facebook. With *My Beloved World*, she revealed herself to be a hardworking girl and woman with a goal. She didn't live a fairy tale life. And yet, her dream came true.

THE RIPPLE EFFECT SINCE THE BOOK RELEASE

In addition to being the best justice she can be, Sonia has three goals: be a good role model, let people know they can aspire to be what they want to be, and teach kids about the law and the Supreme Court.

"The court is a mystery to a lot of people," she said. "I would like there to be no child in America who grows up not knowing what the Supreme Court is." She herself did not know its purpose until she was a student at Princeton and read about how the Supreme Court had ruled that the use of racial quotas was unconstitutional.

In *My Beloved World*, Sotomayor emphasized the fact that there are no perfect people, that even heroes come with blemishes. She opened up about the fear and shame she experienced throughout her childhood and into adulthood. In particular, she referenced the time when some relatives mentioned that her parents' apartment was filthy, with the result that Sonia began paying near obsessive attention to their home's cleanliness.

Staying connected to the community was a promise she made to President Obama and to herself. She wants to show the human side of the justices, but it's not always easy.

"I've felt like an alien because my own family and friends sometimes treated me differently." The first Christmas after she was appointed to the Supreme Court, her family didn't know quite how to react to her. Nobody said a word and were all looking at her until she looked at them and said, "What in the world is wrong with all of you? I'm still Sonia."

And that broke the ice. They screamed, and the shouting and the talking and partying started again, she said.

Sonia's readings created a feeling of celebration. When visiting Puerto Rico during her book tour, she joked that she should be named tourism minister. At the Law School of University of Puerto Rico, people came from all over the island to see her, including an eleven-year-old whose dad accompanied her across the island for hours to get there, and a sixty-seven-year-old man who waited in line eight hours to see her, holding her book the entire time.

But there was something about Sonia that made her connect to people everywhere she went. The Bronx congressman

Jose Serrano said that after her nomination, "people on the street would come running up to me and talk about 'Sonia,' like she's their cousin, or their niece."

It was perhaps why her appearances sold out. People related to her honesty. "There are no excuses to disabilities, diseases, poverty, challenges. If you want to be something, do something purposeful in your life, change your circumstances, it can be done," she said.

In interviews, reporters deem her approachable and less reserved than some of her colleagues. At one appearance to promote her book, she salsa-danced with the Univision anchor Jorge Ramos in her chambers.

Her notoriety put Sonia in the spotlight in other ways. On September 26, 2009, as part of Hispanic Heritage Month outreach, the New York Yankees invited her to throw the first ceremonial pitch at the Yankees vs. Red Sox game. Sonia was a Yankees fan since she was a kid, and Yankee stadium was near her childhood home in the Bronx. She wore the pinstripe jersey when she walked out to the mound and lobbed the baseball down the middle to catcher José Molina. When the Yankees's coach, Joe Girardi, said he'd offer her a contract, she said she'd "stick to my day job."

Remembering her days in the DA's office, Sonia often encouraged attorneys who worked hard but who still occasionally failed to get the recognition she felt they deserved, like The Bronx Defenders. Using a holistic approach for its clients, the organization offered not only legal services with a goal of keeping families together, but also helped with custody, food stamps, and housing issues, and promoted social justice in low-income communities. Sonia attended their events as a show of support.

The "Wise Latina" movement launched the day Sonia took the oath to serve as a Supreme Court justice, and history was made. Women began wearing T-shirts that read, "I am a wise Latina" or "Another Wise Latina Woman" in reference to Sonia's famous line.

The phrase came from a longer quote Sonia had spoken in a 2001 Judge Mario G. Olmos Law and Cultural Diversity Lecture at the University of California, Berkeley: "I would hope that a wise Latina woman with the richness of her experiences would more often than not reach a better conclusion than a white male who hasn't lived that life." Although it drew controversy during her nomination process, she defended and explained the statement.

Latinas saw this as a positive statement and wanted to identify with it, seeing themselves as "Wise Latinas." It was the opportunity to break stereotypes. To show that women are the fastest growing population with economic power in the United States who can educate, who can start businesses, who can help decide the law. Who can become president.

Leticia Van de Putte, a Democratic state senator from San Antonio, Texas, said: "The Honorable Sonia Sotomayor has broken 'the glass ceiling' for all Latinas."

RACE AGAINST THE CLOCK

When Sonia celebrated her fiftieth birthday, she told her friends how she had never expected to live so long. Her diabetes fueled her to make the most of every day. She squeezed all she could out of the days she did have.

A student who enrolled in every extracurricular activity that she could and worked and studied with relentless energy became an adult who kept up that pace in her career, motivated by the feeling that she didn't have very long to live. "I'm past that fear, but I'm not past the lesson it taught," she said.

She considered herself a feminist, but didn't give up hope of finding another life partner after her marriage failed.

It was a fantasy to reach the Supreme Court, a fantasy to swear in the vice president, a fantasy to appear on the *New York Times* bestseller list (especially since Spanish was her first language yet she had somehow mastered and blended her bilingual and bicultural worlds). "My life was no different from so many. To have so many people to be reading a book I authored is incredible."

Most importantly, she reached the goal she'd set when she realized she would never be able to become a law enforcement officer or a private investigator like her novel hero Nancy Drew. Instead, she went on to become the Latina Perry Mason as an attorney in the courtroom, helped right injustices and became a judge. "It is my great hope that I'll be a great justice, and that I'll write opinions that will last the ages. More importantly, it's only one measure of meaning in life. To me, the more important one is my values and my impact on people who feel inspired in any way by me."

THE SOCIAL RESPONSIBILITY

When she took the oath of office for the Supreme Court, memories of running free as a child in the Mayagüez sunshine, with a melting snow cone—a *piragua*—sweet and sticky in her hands, came to mind. "Along with the image, memory carried these words from a child's mind through time: I am blessed."

Maybe she wasn't like the mythological gods she read about in the big book her doctor gave her that helped her through her early childhood days with diabetes. Maybe she wasn't a true rock star.

However, between Latina roots and American pride, Sonia leaves her mark on the world as a justice, judge, lawyer, woman, leader, activist, daughter, and sister. Her promise to carry on the social justice work of Senator Robert Kennedy came to pass.

A witness from the Tarzan Murderer case told her there was something very special about her. The words urged Sonia to keep on her path. At the end of each day she asks herself two questions: What have you learned today? What acts of kindness did you perform? She tells herself: Sonia, you have work to do. Get on with it.

She is "getting on with it." Sonia from the Bronx reached her American dream. As Supreme Court justice of the United States of America, she humbly said, "I think this fish has found her pond."

Appendix A: Awards, Honors, and Recognitions

- The Bronxdale Houses were named after Justice Sotomayor in 2010.

- A portrait named *The Four Justices* by artist Nathan Shanks was created as a tribute of the four trailblazing female Supreme Court justices—Sonia Sotomayor, Ruth Bader Ginsberg, Sandra Day O'Connor, and Elena Kagan. The National Portrait Gallery at the Smithsonian Institute in Washington, D.C., displayed the portrait in 2013.

- Cardinal Spellman Blessed Sacrament school library was named after Sonia Sotomayor.

- The Bronx Defenders honored Justice Sotomayor with the "Partner in Pursuit of Justice" award for her exceptional accomplishments.

- Excerpts from her book, *My Beloved World*, appeared in both *People* and *People en Español* magazines.

- Celebrity status: her former clerk from NYU was Amal Alamuddin, now wife to superstar celebrity actor George Clooney.

- She made the list of "The 75 Most Influential People of the 21st Century" in *Esquire*, 2008.

- In the Los Angeles, California, school district, the Sonia Sotomayor Learning Academies were named after her in 2011.

- She was awarded the *Katherine Hepburn Medal* in 2015 from Bryn Mawr College. The medal "recognizes women who change their worlds: those whose lives, work and contributions embody the intelligence, drive and independence of the four-time Oscar winner and her trailblazing mother. Challenging women to lead publicly engaged lives and to take on important and timely issues affecting women, award recipients are chosen on the basis of their commitment and contributions to civic engagement and the arts."

Appendix B:
Historic Firsts

- Sotomayor was the first Hispanic justice and the first Latina—woman of color—to join the Supreme Court.

- For the first time, inauguration events were scheduled around a book tour. On January 20, she administered the oath of office to Vice President Joseph R. Biden Jr. at the early hour of 8:15 a.m., rather than just before noon as guided by the Constitution, because she had to appear that afternoon at a Barnes & Noble in Manhattan for a book signing.

- Sotomayor came to the U.S. Supreme Court with more federal judicial experience than any justice in a hundred years, and with more overall judicial experience than anyone in 70 years.

- She was the first justice to dance salsa with a reporter during an interview—with Jorge Ramos of Univision.

- She was the first Latina federal judge of the state of New York.

Bibliography

Chapter One
Breaking the Curse

Biskupic, Joan. "Sonia Sotomayor Opens Up About Her Diabetes." *USA Today.*

Children's Diabetes Foundation. http://www.childrensdiabetesfoundation.org/what-is-diabetes/

Diabetes Research Institute. "Diabetes and Kids."

"Forum with Justice Sonia Sotomayor." C-SPAN Video.

Lee, Jolie. "Notable Quotes from Supreme Court's First Latina Justice." *USA Today.* August 8, 2014.

Rawlings, Kelly. "Sonia Sotomayor: Her Life With Diabetes: A candid interview with the Supreme Court justice about her self-care." *Diabetes Forecast.* July 2013.

"Sonia Sotomayor." Biography.com

"Sonia Sotomayor Prefers Sonia from the Bronx." *CBS 60 Minutes.*

Sotomayor, Sonia. *My Beloved World.* Print. 2013.

Totenberg, Nina. "Sonia Sotomayor Opens Up About Diabetes for Youth Group." NPR.

Winter, Jonah. *Sonia Sotomayor: A Judge Grows in the Bronx.* Print.

Wolf, Richard. "Sonia Sotomayor Makes Surprising Revelations in Book." *USA Today.* January 13, 2013.

Chapter Two
Island Girl Values

El Boriqua: Un Poquito de Todo. "Christmas Traditions." A Monthly Bilingual Cultural Publication for Puerto Ricans. http://www.elboricua.com/traditions.html

Fernandez, Manny and Scott Shane. "A Judge's Own Story Highlights Her Mother's." *The New York Times.* Web. May 27, 2009. http://www.nytimes.com/2009/05/28/us/politics/28mother.html?_r=0

Ludden, Jennifer. NPR. "Sotomayor Shaped by her Nuyorican Roots." http://www.npr.org/templates/story/story.php?storyId=105401608

Mayagüez. http://www.prfrogui.com/home/mayaguez.htm. Personal.

Reichard, Raquel. "16 Reasons Why Being Puerto Rican is Best." *Cosmopolitan.* Web. http://www.cosmopolitan.com/lifestyle/news/a38562/why-being-puerto-rican-is-the-best/

Sotomayor, Sonia. "Lecture: A Latina Judge's Voice." *The New York Times.* May 15, 2009.

Sotomayor, Sonia. *My Beloved World.* Print. 2013.

Svoboda, Abigail. "Sonia Sotomayor Knows How to Lead and When to Follow." *The Daily Illini.* Web. http://www.dailyillini.com/article/2016/03/sonia-sotomayor-knows-how-to-lead-and-when-to-follow. March 8, 2016.

Uhrich, Kevin. "Sonia Speaks: An Interview with Justice Sonia Sotomayor." *Progressive*. Web. Feb. 9, 2013. http://www.progressive.org/news/2013/02/180899/sonia-speaks-interview-justice-sonia-sotomayor

U.S. Census Bureau. 2010 data.

Welcome to Puerto Rico. http://welcome.topuertorico.org/city/lajas.shtml

Winfrey, Oprah. "Inspiration: Oprah Talks to Sonia Sotomayor." *O Magazine*. Web. January 28, 2013. http://www.oprah.com/world/Oprah-Interviews-Sonia-Sotomayor-in-O-Magazine

Chapter Three
Sonia from the Bronx

Collins, Laura. *The New Yorker*. Number Nine. Sonia Sotomayor's High-Profile Debut. January 11, 2010. http://www.newyorker.com/magazine/2010/01/11/number-nine

Fernandez, Manny. "The Children at the Judge's Bronx School." *New York Times*. July 15, 2009. http://www.nytimes.com/2009/07/16/nyregion/16bronx.html

Gonzalez, David. "As Her Old School Faces the End, a Justice Reminisces." *New York Times*. Web. January 25, 2013. http://www.nytimes.com/2013/01/26/nyregion/with-her-old-school-set-to-close-a-justice-reminisces.html?_r=0

Ludden, Jennifer. NPR. "Sotomayor Shaped by her Nuyorican Roots." http://www.npr.org/templates/story/story.php?storyId=105401608

NPR. http://www.npr.org/2014/01/13/262067546/as-a-latina-sonia-sotomayor-says-you-have-to-work-harder

Shafy, Samiha. Spiegel Online International. April 2, 2014. http://www.spiegel.de/international/world/interview-with-supreme-court-justice-sonia-sotomayor-a-961986.html

Sotomayor, Sonia. *My Beloved World*. Print. 2013. (co-op).

Stolberg, Sheryl Gay. "Sotomayor, A Trailblazer and a Dreamer." *New York Times*. May 26, 2009.

Uhrich, Kevin. "Sonia Speaks: An Interview with Justice Sonia Sotomayor." *Progressive*. Web. Feb. 9, 2013. http://www.progressive.org/news/2013/02/180899/sonia-speaks-interview-justice-sonia-sotomayor

U.S. Census.

Chapter Four
Star Student: Launching the American Dream

Fernandez, Manny. "The Children at the Judge's Bronx School." *New York Times*. July 15, 2009. http://www.nytimes.com/2009/07/16/nyregion/16bronx.html

Gonzalez, David. "As Her Old School Faces the End, a Justice Reminisces." *New York Times*. Web. January 25, 2013. http://www.nytimes.com/2013/01/26/nyregion/with-her-old-school-set-to-close-a-justice-reminisces.html?_r=0

Iasevoli, Brenda. "A Judge Like No Other." *Time for Kids*. Sept. 18, 2009. Web. http://www.timeforkids.com/news/justice-no-other/171201

Ludden, Jennifer. NPR. "Sotomayor Shaped by her Nuyorican Roots." http://www.npr.org/templates/story/story.php?storyId=105401608

Pitney, Nico. "Sonia Sotomayor, Supreme Court Nominee: All You Need to Know." *Huffington Post*. May 25, 2011. http://www.huffingtonpost.com/2009/05/01/sonia-sotomayor-supreme-c_n_194470.html

Sotomayor, Sonia. *My Beloved World*. Print. 2013.

Stolberg, Sheryl Gay. "Sotomayor, A Trailblazer and a Dreamer." *New York Times*. May 26, 2009.

Svoboda, Abigail. "Sonia Sotomayor Knows How to Lead and When to Follow." *The Daily Illini*. Web. http://www.dailyillini.com/article/2016/03/sonia-sotomayor-knows-how-to-lead-and-when-to-follow. March 8, 2016.

Uhrich, Kevin. "Sonia Speaks: An Interview with Justice Sonia Sotomayor." *Progressive*. Web. Feb. 9, 2013. http://www.progressive.org/news/2013/02/180899/sonia-speaks-interview-justice-sonia-sotomayor

Chapter Five
The Fairy Tale Land of the Ivy League

Biography.com. "Sonia Sotomayor." Web.

Discover the Networks. "Individual Profile: Sonia Sotomayor." Web. 2009. http://www.discoverthenetworks.org/individualProfile.asp?indid=2396

Frazier, Ian. *The New Yorker*. "Sonia from the Bronx." Feb. 8 & 15, 2016. http://www.newyorker.com/magazine/2016/02/08/sonia-from-the-bronx

Investopedia. "What is the Difference Between Magna Cum Laude and Summa Cum Laude?" June 3, 2016. Web. http://www.investopedia.com/ask/answers/032415/what-difference-between-magnum-cum-laude-and-summa-cum-laude.asp

Ludden, Jennifer. NPR. "Sotomayor Shaped by her Nuyorican Roots." http://www.npr.org/templates/story/story.php?storyId=105401608

NPR. http://www.npr.org/2014/01/13/262067546/as-a-latina-sonia-sotomayor-says-you-have-to-work-harder

Princeton University. "About Princeton: Overview." Web. http://www.princeton.edu/main/about/

Rubenstone, Sally. "What Constitutes Ivy League?" Ask the Dean. Web. http://www.collegeconfidential.com/dean/000054/

Sotomayor, Sonia. *My Beloved World*. Print. 2013.

Stolberg, Sheryl Gay. "Sotomayor, A Trailblazer and a Dreamer." *New York Times*. May 26, 2009.

Uhrich, Kevin. "Sonia Speaks: An Interview with Justice Sonia Sotomayor." *Progressive*. Web. Feb. 9, 2013. http://www.progressive.org/news/2013/02/180899/sonia-speaks-interview-justice-sonia-sotomayor

U.S. Supreme Court Case Tracker. Supreme Court Review. "Updates on Our Nation's Highest Court: 2015-2016 Term." Web. http://supremecourtreview.com/default/justice/index/id/45

Yale University. U.S. Supreme Court Justice Sonia Sotomayor Visits Yale. YouTube. Video. Feb. 12, 2014. Web. https://www.youtube.com/watch?v=8ODnaFRc_mM

Chapter Six
One Step Closer to a Latina Perry Mason

Fernandez, Manny. "The Children at the Judge's Bronx School." *New York Times.* July 15, 2009. http://www.nytimes.com/2009/07/16/nyregion/16bronx.html

Ford, Matt. "Pleading for the Fourth." *The Atlantic.* Web. November 12, 2015. http://www.theatlantic.com/politics/archive/2015/11/justice-sotomayor-fourth-amendment/414948/

Frazier, Ian. *The New Yorker.* "Sonia from the Bronx." Feb. 8 & 15, 2016. http://www.newyorker.com/magazine/2016/02/08/sonia-from-the-bronx

Gonzalez, David. "As Her Old School Faces the End, a Justice Reminisces." *New York Times.* Web. January 25, 2013. http://www.nytimes.com/2013/01/26/nyregion/with-her-old-school-set-to-close-a-justice-reminisces.html?_r=0

Ludden, Jennifer. NPR. "Sotomayor Shaped by her Nuyorican Roots." http://www.npr.org/templates/story/story.php?storyId=105401608

Miller, Elizabeth. Santa Fe Reporter. "Still Tilting at Windmills: Associate Justice Sonia Sotomayor speaks to the books that inspired her, and the work that continues." Web. http://www.sfreporter.com/santafe/article-11812-%E2%80%98still-tilting-at-windmills%E2%80%99.html

Safranek, Lynn. "A Special Day with Justice Sotomayor." *The Record Alumni Magazine,* The University of Chicago, The Law School. Spring 2011. Web. http://www.law.uchicago.edu/alumni/magazine/spring11/sotomayor

Sotomayor, Sonia. *My Beloved World.* Print. 2013.

Sterbenz, Christina. "Here's What it Takes to Get into America's Best Law Schools." Business Insider.org. Web. August 13, 2013. http://www.businessinsider.com/qualifications-for-top-tier-law-schools-2013-7

"The Supreme Court: What Does it Do?" U.S. History.org. Web. http://www.ushistory.org/gov/9c.asp

Yale University. U.S. Supreme Court Justice Sonia Sotomayor Visits Yale. YouTube. Video. Feb. 12, 2014. Web. https://www.youtube.com/watch?v=8ODnaFRc_mM

Chapter Seven
Seeking Justice for All in the Courtroom

Collins, Lauren. "Number Nine: Sonia Sotomayor's High Profile Debut." *The New Yorker.* January 11, 2010. Web. http://www.newyorker.com/magazine/2010/01/11/number-nine

Frazier, Ian. "Sonia from the Bronx." *The New Yorker.* February 8 & 15, 2016. http://www.newyorker.com/magazine/2016/02/08/sonia-from-the-bronx

Infoplease.com. Biography, Sonia Sotomayor. http://www.infoplease.com/biography/var/soniasotomayor.html

Mueller, Benjamin. "For Immigration Lawyers, a Surprise Speaker Who Asks Them to Change Lives; Sonia Sotomayor Speaks to Immigrant Justice Corps." *The New York Times.* September 4, 2014. Web. http://www.nytimes.com/2014/09/05/nyregion/for-immigration-lawyers-a-surprise-speaker-justice-sonia-sotomayor-of-the-supreme-court.html?_r=1

Social Studies for Kids. "Justice Sonia Sotomayor." http://www.socialstudiesforkids.com/articles/government/sotomayor.htm

Safranek, Lynn. "A Special Day with Justice Sotomayor." *The Record Alumni Magazine*, The University of Chicago, The Law School. Spring 2011. Web. http://www.law. uchicago.edu/alumni/magazine/spring11/sotomayor

Sotomayor, Sonia. *My Beloved World*. Print. 2013.

Stolberg, Sheryl Gay. "Sotomayor, A Trailblazer and a Dreamer." *New York Times*. May 26, 2009.

Supreme Court Review. Updates on Our Nation's Highest Court. http://supremecourtreview. com/default/justice/index/id/45

"U.S. Supreme Court Associate Justice Sonia Sotomayor Speaks at The Bronx Defenders." *The Bronx Defenders*. January 29, 2016. Web.

U.S. Supreme Court Case Tracker: Supreme Court Review: Updates on Our Nation's Highest Court 2015-2016 Term. http://supremecourtreview.com/default/justice/index/id/45

Chapter Eight
Slipping into the Black Robes

Collins, Laura. *The New Yorker*. Number Nine. Sonia Sotomayor's High-Profile Debut. January 11, 2010. http://www.newyorker.com/magazine/2010/01/11/number-nine

Coto, Danica. Associated Press. NBC Latino. "Sotomayor Draws Hundreds in Puerto Rico for Book Tour." April 3, 2013. Web. http://nbclatino.com/2013/04/03/sotomayor-draws-hundreds-in-puerto-rico-for-book-tour/

HSF Stories.

Ludden, Jennifer. NPR. "Sotomayor Shaped by her Nuyorican Roots." http://www.npr.org/ templates/story/story.php?storyId=105401608

Sotomayor, Sonia. *My Beloved World*. Print. 2013.

Stolberg, Sheryl Gay. "Sotomayor, A Trailblazer and a Dreamer." *New York Times*. May 26, 2009.

U.S. Supreme Court Case Tracker: Supreme Court Review: Updates on Our Nation's Highest Court 2015-2016 Term. http://supremecourtreview.com/default/justice/index/id/45

Chapter Nine
Sonia Style: Making Her Way to the Supreme Court

Collins, Laura. *The New Yorker*. Number Nine. Sonia Sotomayor's High-Profile Debut. January 11, 2010. http://www.newyorker.com/magazine/2010/01/11/number-nine

Gregory, Sean. *Time Magazine*. "How Sotomayor 'Saved' Baseball." Web. May 26, 2009. http://content.time.com/time/nation/article/0,8599,1900974,00.html

Miller, Elizabeth. Santa Fe Reporter. "Still Tilting at Windmills: Associate Justice Sonia Sotomayor speaks to the books that inspired her, and the work that continues." Web. http://www.sfreporter.com/santafe/article-11812-%E2%80%98still-tilting-at-windmills%E2%80%99.html

NPR. "As a Latina, Sotomayor Says You Have to Work Harder." Web. http://www.npr. org/2014/01/13/262067546/as-a-latina-sonia-sotomayor-says-you-have-to-work-harder

Patel, Ushma. *Princeton News*. "Sotomayor Shares Insights on Journey to the Supreme Court." April 30, 2011. Web. https://www.princeton.edu/main/news/archive/S30/41/33S56/index.xml

Savage, Charlie. *The New York Times*. "Sotomayor Sworn in as Supreme Court Justice."
    August 8, 2009. Web. http://www.nytimes.com/2009/08/09/us/politics/09sotomayor.
    html?_r=2
Sotomayor, Sonia. *My Beloved World*. Print. 2013.
Shafy, Samiha. Spiegel Online International. April 2, 2014. http://www.spiegel.de/interna-
    tional/world/interview-with-supreme-court-justice-sonia-sotomayor-a-961986.html
Stolberg, Sheryl Gay. "Sotomayor, a Trailblazer and a Dreamer." *New York Times*. May 26,
    2009.

Chapter Ten
The People's Justice

Architecture.about.com. U.S. Supreme Court Building: Main Entrance. Web.
Associated Press. Sotomayor Sworn in as Supreme Court Justice. Nbcnews.com. August
    8, 2009. Web. http://www.nbcnews.com/id/32340419/ns/politics-supreme_court/t/
    sotomayor-sworn-supreme-court-justice/#.VxQNpfkrKUl
Biskupic, Joan. *USA Today*. "Oyez! Oyez! Court Set for Sotomayor Ceremony." September
    7, 2009. Web. http://usatoday30.usatoday.com/news/washington/judicial/2009-09-07-
    sotomayor_N.htm
FarmersAlmanac.com. "Weather History Results for Washington, D.C.; August 9, 2009."
    Web.
Frazier, Ian. "Sonia from the Bronx." *The New Yorker*. February 8 & 15. Web. http://www.
    newyorker.com/magazine/2016/02/08/sonia-from-the-bronx
Hispanic Scholarship Fund. Latina Stories.
Ludden, Jennifer. NPR. "Sotomayor Shaped by her Nuyorican Roots." http://www.npr.org/
    templates/story/story.php?storyId=105401608
National Centers for Environmental Information. "Climate at a Glance: District of
    Columbia." Web. http://www.ncdc.noaa.gov/cag/time-series/us/49/USW00093738/
    tmin/1/8/2009-2009?base_prd=true&firstbaseyear=1901&lastbaseyear=2000
Navarro, Mireya. *The New York Times*. "Sotomayor Fans Claim the Phrase 'Wise Latina."
    August 7, 2009. http://www.nytimes.com/2009/08/09/fashion/09latina.html?action=cli
    ck&contentCollection=Politics&module=RelatedCoverage&region=EndOfArticle&pgt
    ype=article
Patel, Ushma. *Princeton News*. "Sotomayor Shares Insights on Journey to the Supreme
    Court." April 30, 2011. Web. https://www.princeton.edu/main/news/archive/
    S30/41/33S56/index.xml
"Sonia Sotomayor." *Oyez*. Chicago-Kent College of Law at Illinois Tech, n.d. Apr 29, 2016.
    https://www.oyez.org/justices/sonia_sotomayor
Sotomayor, Sonia. *My Beloved World*. Print. 2013.
Stolberg, Sheryl Gay. "Sotomayor, a Trailblazer and a Dreamer." *New York Times*. May 26,
    2009.
SupremeCourt.gov. Frequently Asked Questions (FAQs). Web.
Uhrich, Kevin. "Sonia Speaks: An Interview with Justice Sonia Sotomayor." *Progressive*. Web.
    Feb. 9, 2013. http://www.progressive.org/news/2013/02/180899/sonia-speaks-interview-
    justice-sonia-sotomayor

U.S. Supreme Court Case Tracker: Supreme Court Review: Updates on Our Nation's Highest Court 2015-2016 Term. http://supremecourtreview.com/default/justice/index/id/45
"What does the Supreme Court Do? The Judicial Branch: American Government. Web. http://www.ushistory.org/gov/9c.asp

Chapter Eleven
The Rock Star Life

Coto, Danica. *Associated Press*. NBC Latino. "Sotomayor Draws Hundreds in Puerto Rico for Book Tour." April 3, 2013. Web. http://nbclatino.com/2013/04/03/sotomayor-draws-hundreds-in-puerto-rico-for-book-tour/

Fernandez, Manny. "The Children at the Judge's Bronx School." *New York Times.* July 15, 2009. http://www.nytimes.com/2009/07/16/nyregion/16bronx.html

Kantor, Jodi. *The New York Times.* On Book-Tour Circuit, Sotomayor Sees a New Niche for a Justice. Feb. 3, 2013. Web. http://www.nytimes.com/2013/02/04/us/politics/book-tour-rock-star-sotomayor-sees-an-even-higher-calling.html?_r=0

Gonzalez, David. "As Her Old School Faces the End, a Justice Reminisces." *New York Times.* Web. January 25, 2013. http://www.nytimes.com/2013/01/26/nyregion/with-her-old-

Latino Leaders Staff. "15 Most Powerful Latinas: They are the Alpha Females. The Latina Leaders Magazine's A-List of the Most Influential Hispanic Women in America. Web. May 2015. http://www.latinoleaders.com/February-March-2015/15-Most-Powerful-Latinas.

Latino USA. "Sonia Sotomayor's Beloved World." April 8, 2016. http://latinousa. org/2016/04/08/sonia-sotomayors-beloved-world/ (original 2013 interview revisited)

Lilley, Sandra. NBC Latino. "In Memoir, Sonia Sotomayor Reveals Childhood Struggles and Fighting Spirit." January 14, 2013. Web. http://nbclatino.com/2013/01/14/in-memoir-sonia-sotomayor-reveals-childhood-struggles-and-fighting-spirit/

Miller, Elizabeth. Santa Fe Reporter. "'Still tilting at windmills' Associate Justice Sonia Sotomayor speaks to the books that inspired her, and the work that continues." April 7, 2016. Web. http://www.sfreporter.com/santafe/article-11812-%E2%80%98still-tilting-at-windmills%E2%80%99.html

Roman, Elizabeth. Masslive.com. "Justice Sonia Sotomayor Inspires Crowd in Springfield, Shares Childhood Stories." September 9, 2015. http://www.masslive.com/news/index. ssf/2015/09/sonia_sotomayor_inspires.html

Safranek, Lynn. "A Special Day with Justice Sotomayor." *The Record Alumni Magazine*, The University of Chicago, The Law School. Spring 2011. Web. http://www.law.uchicago.edu/ alumni/magazine/spring11/sotomayor

SoCalConnected. KCET. "Justice Sonia Sotomayor Talks Struggle, Success with Actress Eva Longoria." Web. January 26, 2013. https://www.kcet.org/search?query=shows%20 socal%20connected%20content%20interview%20justice%20sonia%20sotomayor%20 talks%20struggle%20success%20with%20actress%20eva%20longoria

Sotomayor, Sonia. *My Beloved World*. 2013. Print.

U.S. Supreme Court Case Tracker: Supreme Court Review: Updates on Our Nation's Highest Court 2015-2016 Term. http://supremecourtreview.com/default/justice/index/id/45

About the Author

Sylvia Mendoza motivates young audiences with true stories about the early lives of trailblazing women and men. She is the author of *The Book of Latina Women: 150 Vidas of Passion, Strength, and Success* (2004). Her work was chosen for the California Collection for High Schools by the California Readers Association, won first place in the International Latino Book Awards, and was featured by the National Women's History Project in a program broadcast on C-Span's Book-TV.